Unheard Story

Also by Pádraig McCarthy

A Wedding of Your Own. Veritas, 1978, 2003.
My Name Is Patrick. Royal Irish Academy, 2011.

Unheard Story

Dublin Archdiocese and *The Murphy Report*

Pádraig McCarthy

First published in 2013
by Londubh Books
18 Casimir Avenue, Harold's Cross, Dublin 6w, Ireland
www.londubh.ie
1 3 5 4 2
Layout by Londubh Books in Garamond and Myriad Pro; cover by bluett
Printed in Dublin by SprintPrint
ISBN: 978-1-907535-35-2

Contents

Acknowledgements

I would like to acknowledge my debt in the writing of this book to the Association of Catholic Priests (ACP) and specifically to the group under its auspices that has been studying the complex matter of how child sexual abuse has been handled.

In particular I acknowledge the work of retired judge, Fergal Sweeney, in his study: *Commissions of Investigation and Procedural Fairness: A Review from a Legal Perspective of the Commissions of Investigation Act 2004 and of the Report into the Catholic Archdiocese of Dublin (The Murphy Report)*.

This study will released by the ACP at the same time as this book. See www.associationofcatholicpriests.ie.

I acknowledge the kind permission of *The Furrow* to reproduce (Appendix IV and Appendix V) two articles published in 2010 and 2012.

I also want to acknowledge the willing assistance of Jo O'Donoghue of Londubh Books in tackling the design, editing and publication of the present book, all in a most unreasonable time frame! This has taken an enormous burden off my shoulders.

Foreword by Seán McDonagh

This book by Pádraig McCarthy, examining *The Murphy Report* four years after its publication, is timely and very courageous. When the report was published in November 2009, it was immediately embraced by the media and even by some Church leaders as the definitive word on how the sexual abuse of minors by priests had been handled in the Church. I think it is no exaggeration to say that the document was given almost infallible status. It also provoked widespread anger, much of it directed at the Church officials who were mentioned in the document. But there was also a wave of anger against the Catholic Church itself. An editorial in *The Irish Times* on 27 November 2009 claimed that 'denial and cover-up was the order of the day...the vast majority of uninvolved priests turned a blind eye. As might be expected, given the traditional supine attitude of governments to the Catholic hierarchy, state agencies avoided involvement. It would be wrong to conclude that criminal behaviour by priests in Dublin archdiocese was exceptional.'

In his book, Pádraig McCarthy challenges these claims. He shows clearly that the claim that a 'vast majority of uninvolved priests turned a blind eye' to the abuse is based on a badly written paragraph in *The Murphy Report* (1.24) which states that 'some priests were aware that particular instances of abuse had occurred'. A commission of investigation that was set up by the Oireachtas to give us data, not opinions, should have told us how many priests knew – was it ten or was it a hundred? – and how they came by the information. When such a commission makes an accusation as serious as this, numbers matter. The paragraph continues: 'A few were courageous and brought complaints to the attention of their superiors.' We may still be dealing with a relatively small number of people but the next sentence cuts lose and effectively tars and feathers every priest in the Dublin archdiocese by claiming that 'the vast majority simply chose to turn a blind eye'. It is preposterous to claim, without any concrete data by way of survey, that the vast majority of the four hundred and thirteen priests who are serving in the archdiocese of Dublin in September 2013 knew about the abuse perpetrated by a small number of their colleagues. If any other profession were treated as incompetently and shabbily as the priests of the Dublin archdiocese there would have been vociferous demands either for conclusive proof of the accusation or that it should be withdrawn immediately. Instead, it became grist for the mill of *The Irish Times* editorial.

Right through the book, the author emphasises that he is not claiming that there was no sexual abuse of children by clergy or that complaints were always handled in a competent and child-friendly way. He is extremely sensitive to the pain and trauma the victims and their families suffered and the long-term negative impact of abuse on the lives of the victims. Victims and their families rightly believe that *The Murphy Report* increased the awareness of child sexual abuse in Ireland and helped to bring about a safer society and a safer Church. Neither is he claiming that there was a parity of pain and hurt between the victims of abuse and those who might have suffered by having their names mentioned by the commission of investigation. Clearly this is not the case but two wrongs do not make something right.

What Pádraig McCarthy is doing is challenging some of the underlying assumptions of the Murphy Commission, which completely rejected the testimony of many of the diocesan officials who had to deal with priests who had abused children over the previous few decades. The officials readily admitted that, viewed through the prism of our knowledge of paedophilia in 2009, they made serious mistakes in returning priests who had abused to ministry. But these officials claimed that they were on a 'learning curve' and that the advice they received from professional counsellors or psychologists, when viewed in the light of our present knowledge, was very flawed. *The Murphy Report* categorically rejects the claim that diocesan officials were on any such 'learning curve'.

McCarthy examines and challenges the arguments used to support this assertion. This was a commission of investigation so it could easily have settled the question of whether or not there was a 'learning curve' by sifting through relevant data. Researchers for the commission could have examined textbooks and journal articles on moral theology, counselling, psychology and psychiatry running from the mid-1960s to the mid-1990s. If they had discovered that our current knowledge of paedophilia and its impact on the lives of the victims was well known in the early 1960s, the report could rightfully have claimed that there was no 'learning curve'. But McCarthy makes it clear that such knowledge was not available to government agencies or social workers until the late 1980s. The 1975 expert group established by the Department of Health to establish the extent of the problem of non-accidental injuries to children makes no reference to the sexual abuse of children. Social workers told the commission that awareness of child sexual abuse did not emerge in Ireland until the early 1980s.

Dr G.P. Lewis highlights this lack of historical perspective in the report in a letter to the editor of *The Irish Times* (17 December 2009). He is not saying that Church authorities had not made serious mistakes – mistakes that had appalling consequences for those who were abused – but he claims that they were 'made in the context of the time'. It is worth quoting what he wrote at length: 'Less than twenty years ago most educated people had never heard the word "paedophilia". As far as I am aware, professional and statutory bodies did not know how to deal with the problem when it arose. The judiciary would give out suspended sentences with a warning to offenders. The social services and the Gardaí would often ignore information given to them of allegations of child sexual abuse in their area. They were extremely hesitant to intrude into the privacy of a family where such abuse might be happening. The psychological/psychiatric professions sent offenders on treatment programmes and would often certify such people back to their location, or ministry in the case of priests, not realising that a very high percentage re-offended…It was only fifteen years ago, when survivors felt free to tell their stories and be heard in the process, that it finally dawned on society – and not just the Church – how appalling a crime sexual abuse is and the great damage it does. Of course, one can say that the leaders in the Catholic Church should have known better but in the context of the time they unfortunately did not. They failed – as other professions failed likewise.'

The Murphy Report and many media and religious comment-ators wrongly dismissed this account of the growth in our understanding of paedophilia as fiction. If the commission had employed a historian she/he would have verified the above scenario as the historical truth.

McCarthy challenges the report's blanket accusation that 'the commission has no doubt but that clerical child sexual abuse was covered up by the archdiocese of Dublin and other Church authorities over much of the period covered by the commission's remit.' He challenges this assertion even in regard to the way officials of the archdiocese of Dublin, including Archbishop Dermot Ryan, dealt with the case of Patrick McCabe. *The Murphy Report* states categorically that the McCabe case 'encapsulates everything that was wrong with the Archdiocesan handling of child sexual abuse cases.' McCarthy, having sifted through the data in the report itself, claims that 'Chapter 20 [which deals with the Patrick McCabe case] encapsulates very much what was right in the archdiocesan handling of child sexual abuse cases. It also encapsulates much of what was wrong with the commission's implementation of its mandate.'

This unchallenged generalisation by the commission allowed the media to make all kinds of exaggerated claims, based on flimsy data. In an Opinion article in *The Irish Times* on 30 July 2013 entitled 'Ten socially destructive acts to commit with impunity', Fintan O'Toole gave as an example the 'covering up and repeatedly facilitating sexual attacks on children by known predatory paedophiles' by several Irish bishops.

McCarthy has done an excellent job in raising serious questions about crucial aspects of *The Murphy Report*. But there are also legal aspects of the report and the legislation that underpinned it that need to be addressed if similar commissions of investigation are going to be used by the government in the future.

During the second reading of the Commissions of Investigation Bill 2003 on 4 March 2004, opposition spokespeople raised serious questions about the rights to due process and fair procedures that are enshrined in the legislation. M.J. O'Keefe of Fine Gael pointed out: 'We must ask if the Bill strikes the right balance. Article 40.3.20 of the Constitution grants each person the right to a good name and the protection of this right before the courts necessitates the right of representation, particularly when one's good name may be called into question. As the tribunal system and the proposed commission system is, despite the best efforts of the minister, somewhat adversarial in nature, questions are asked and answers given that often attribute responsibility to someone else. If, in a private hearing, a person is not aware of the adverse comments through a denial of representation, are his or her constitutional rights being violated? We must consider these issues now before the Bill is enacted.'

Deputy Joe Costello of the Labour Party had similar reservations. He said: 'the points Deputy O'Keefe and I are presenting here are fairly important. It is not enough for the section to state that the commission will adhere to "fair procedures", as is stated at the top of the page. One must also incorporate them into the legislation. All that is allowed a person under Subsection 3 is 'an opportunity to comment' by written or oral submission on the evidence.

Deputy Michael Smith, who was taking questions for Minister Michael McDowell, assured Deputy O'Keefe that the right balance had been struck and rejected the amendment. I believe this was a mistake and, having read Padraig McCarthy's book and sections 1.49, 1.51 and 1.53 of *The Murphy Report,* I think that one could make a very plausible case that Bishop Dermot O'Mahony's and Bishop Donal Murray's constitutional right to their good name were compromised. The reputational damage done to Bishop Murray was a fundamental element in his decision to resign as bishop of Limerick.

Given the fact that fair procedures were circumvented, lawyers might also ask whether the Murphy Commission had a right to mention any individual by name in the report. Should it have confined itself to identifying systemic failures in the institutions that were under scrutiny? Given the appalling reality of child sex abuse it is understandable that the public would wish to see those who they think were responsible for not protecting children named, shamed and even gaoled. But this is the logic of the lynching mob. The reason we have laws and courts and a commitment to due process in civilised countries is to protect the innocent and to convict those who are guilty. But the level of proof has to be serious – beyond reasonable doubt in criminal courts.

Social scientists might also examine the value and fairness of focusing on a single profession without having a control group against which to judge the behaviour of the group being studied. If the commission had assessed how Garda authorities handled child sex abuse allegations among the members of the Garda Síochána, realistic comparisons might have been possible, as well as establishing why one group was better than the other. The reasons might have been that the Gardaí had a better reporting system or, perhaps, a better educational programme for dealing with sex abuse. Without such comparative data it is very easy to scapegoat the group that is being studied.

A nationwide survey of 1000 Irish people carried out by Amárach Research in September 2011 found that the majority of the public overestimated the number of Catholic clergy who have been guilty of child sex abuse. In response to the question: 'In your opinion, approximately what percentage of Irish priests are guilty of child abuse?', more than 21 per cent of respondents stated that 42 per cent of priests were guilty of abusing children. The most authoritative estimate to date, produced by the John Jay College of Criminal Justice in the US, puts the true number of a priests accused of paedophilia at 4 per cent.

Commenting on the findings on behalf of the Iona Institute, Professor Patricia Casey said: 'There has been very deep and completely justified public anger over the scandal of child sex abuse by clergy. However, only a small minority of priests are guilty of this terrible crime and in the interests of justice and in fairness to the vast majority of priests, it is essential that this fact becomes universally known among the public at large.'

A faulty perception by the public that priests are more likely to sexually abuse children than other males will not help protect vulnerable children. International and national data make it clear that the vast majority of instances of sex abuse of children take place within the family and is perpetrated by a family member or a friend of the family. Policies to protect children from abuse must reflect this data. Transferring blame to one small group will not help vulnerable children.

At the beginning I said that Pádraig McCarthy showed courage in writing this book. The abuse of children is abhorrent and appalling, particularly when perpetrated by priests whose vocation is to nurture faith and love in the community of Church. The attitude of Jesus welcoming children should be the norm for priests (*Luke* 18:15). It is wrong and seriously sinful when such trust is broken and children are harmed, often for the rest of their lives. Their stories were vindicated by *The Murphy Report* and this is to be welcomed and celebrated.

Discussions around the abuse of children are, understandably, often highly charged, as so much pain and hurt has been experienced. As a result, anyone raising a question about the conclusions of *The Murphy Report* can easily be portrayed as being insensitive to the pain caused by the sexual abuse of children by priests. But, as this book makes clear, the truth is much more complex and, in the long run, a society is much better served by knowing all the facts, rather than being presented with a lopsided version of the past. Only by diligently sifting through the evidence, as McCarthy has done, can we come to a better understanding of the truth, which will enable us to devise better policies for children and other vulnerable people. The author makes no exaggerated claims for his work and states that he is willing to acknowledge any errors in the book.

All I ask is that readers, especially those who uncritically embraced *The Murphy Report* in November 2009, receive McCarthy's book with an open mind. If they do, I think they will have a much more balanced view of the strengths and weaknesses of the report.

Seán McDonagh is a member of the leadership team
of the Association of Catholic Priests (ACP).

Introduction

This purpose of this book is to examine critically the report of the commission of investigation established in 2006 to enquire into handling of allegations of sexual abuse of children by clergy serving in the diocese of Dublin. While recognising what is valuable, it suggests that a serious reassessment of the report's conclusions is needed.

The report is usually referred to as *The Murphy Report,* because the commission was headed by Judge Yvonne Murphy. The website of the Murphy Commission lists the three members of the commission. As well as Judge Murphy (chairperson), there were Ita Mangan and Hugh O'Neill. Maeve Doherty was the solicitor to the commission.

The opening paragraph of the report (1.1) clearly states the scope of the task of the commission: 'The Dublin Archdiocese Commission of Investigation was established to report on the handling by Church and State authorities of a representative sample of allegations and suspicions of child sexual abuse against clerics operating under the aegis of the archdiocese of Dublin over the period 1975 to 2004.'

My reason for writing *Unheard Story* is that the report has, until now, received almost universal acceptance and there has been little analysis of how the commission arrived at its assessments and conclusions. I welcome the vindication the report provided for the many people who were abused by priests in the diocese of Dublin and recognise that the handling of allegations by Church and state authorities in many cases did not meet the standard we would now expect. The question I address is whether the conclusions of the report are consistent with the facts.

Sexual abuse of children is a deeply emotional topic, especially for those who were subjected to the hurt and injustice of being abused as children. It also arouses a great deal of anger: anger with those who inflicted the abuse and anger with those in church and state who, for whatever reason, failed to deal effectively with the allegations. This book recognises the very deep and long-lasting effects of such abuse, which we have come to understand better in recent years, and I hope it will contribute to a deepening of our understanding, thereby helping the healing process.

This is a summary of the arguments I present in an attempt to set the record straight:

1. *The Murphy Report* about the handling by church and state authorities of allegations of sexual abuse of children by clergy serving in the diocese of Dublin has helped to validate stories of people abused and has raised the level of public awareness of such abuse in Irish society.
2. *The Murphy Report* has been uncritically accepted and acclaimed, without serious examination.
3. Courts administer justice in public. The work of this commission of investigation was not public.
4. The report assesses the handling of allegations of child sexual abuse. In twenty-seven cases it approves the handling of allegations by the diocese; in eighteen cases it criticises it.
5. To question the findings of the report does not imply casting doubt on the terrible reality of abuse that did take place. Nor does it imply that handling of allegations was all that we would expect today.
6. The report rejects the claim by diocesan officials that they were on a learning curve prior to the late 1990s, something that greatly damages their credibility, but it does not provide evidence to support this rejection.
7. Chapter 20 contains many errors. The commission claims at the close of this chapter that this case encapsulates all that

was wrong in the diocese's handling of complaints but the evidence of the chapter itself shows quite the opposite. The fact that so many of the diocese's efforts resulted in failure was not a result of negligence. At that time, nobody had the answer.

8. Chapter 20 names nineteen diocesan officials with responsibility in the handling of allegations but state officials involved remain anonymous. This requires explanation.

9. The allegation that the diocese engaged in a nefarious 'cover-up' oversimplifies a very complex situation and is not in accordance with the facts.

10. The categorical nature of the assessments by the commission is attractive and seems to meet the need for a response to the great injury and injustice of the sexual abuse of children but it is dangerous in that it can distract us from rationally considering the evidence.

11. The report fails badly in not taking account of the level of knowledge and understanding in the historically different, although relatively recent decades in question; in not seeing the facts in the context of the problem of abuse in Irish society; and in not relating the findings to how sexual abuse of children was handled by other organisations.

12. The fact that bishops and other officials did not fight back and that some resigned is not in itself evidence of guilt: other factors were involved.

13. The Murphy Commission, in trying to deal effectively with a horrifying and difficult reality, may possibly have fallen into human error.

14. The media's uncritical acceptance of the report has helped create a public perception not in accordance with the facts.

The Murphy Commission website states: 'The commission has completed its investigation into the Dublin Archdiocese and the

Catholic Diocese of Cloyne. The commission is now closed.' When I refer in this book to the commission of investigation or *The Murphy Report,* I am referring only to the Dublin investigation.

I wrote this book entirely on my own initiative. No person or organisation commissioned me or requested me to write it. I accept full responsibility for its content but I would like to thank friends who read the book in manuscript form and made helpful suggestions. I welcome any comments on the assessment I provide in *Unheard Story.* Please email them to murphyreportcomments@gmail.com.

Pádraig McCarthy,
Dublin, October 2013

Note

The Irish word 'Garda' (properly *Garda Síochána,* guardians of the peace) designates the Irish police force; 'Gardaí' are the members of the force.

1

A Priest of the Dublin Archdiocese

After I was ordained in 1967 for service in Dublin archdiocese, my first appointment was as chaplain to Artane Industrial School for Boys in Dublin. It is well known for the 'Artane Boys' Band' which plays regularly at matches in Croke Park.

I had absolutely no experience or training in this kind of work; nor was I given any information or training at the time. I learned quickly that the boys in the school had quite a different experience of family life from what I had known growing up. My predecessor as chaplain in Artane had written a report about harsh conditions in the school for Archbishop John Charles McQuaid in 1962 and this resulted in improvements. I was not given a copy of the report, nor was I informed of its existence. I did not discover its existence until more than thirty years later.

This report made no mention of sexual abuse but my predecessor did write: 'The very structure of the school is in dilapidated condition, colourless and uninspiring and reflects the interior spirit...The atmosphere is somewhat unreal, particularly in regard to lack of contact with the opposite sex and this unnatural situation in a group of 450 boys plus a staff of forty men invariably leads to a degree of sexual maladjustment in the boys...I strongly recommend the introduction of female personnel.' There was a community of nuns working in Artane when I started in 1967.

I discovered that a course in childcare was about to begin, organised by CYCG (Child and Youth Care Group), in the Diocesan Institute of Adult Education in Eccles St, Dublin. This was to run on Saturdays from September 1967 to the following Easter. I enrolled for this course. It was a time of significant changeover from large institutions to smaller home-type care so the course involved visits to a number of care homes in the Dublin area and I learned a lot from it.

Throughout that course, there was no mention whatsoever of sexual abuse of children. Indeed, until the 1990s, I would never have thought of such abuse. In my ten months or so in Artane, I never encountered any abuse of the boys, except for one incident when, while speaking to one Christian Brother, I noticed some distance away another Brother striking a boy on the head. It was something I had never seen in my nine years attending the CBS in Synge Street. (This, remember, was 1968 and corporal punishment in schools was common; the ban on corporal punishment did not come until 1982.) I honestly do not know what I would have done if it had continued but this did not arise: it was one isolated incident that I witnessed.

The week the course concluded, I received a new appointment to the parish of St Pius X in Templeogue.

I had some limited contact with Father Patrick McCabe, whose history as a child-abuser is the subject of the recently released Chapter 20 of *The Murphy Report*. He was in his final year in Clonliffe when I started there in 1960; he was a likeable figure but we had little interaction. He was ordained in 1961. While I was serving in the parish of St Brigid in Killester 1978-1985, he was in the neighbouring parish of Artane. I once had occasion to call to his house and saw his prayer room, in what would have been a front bedroom. I saw nothing untoward. I was interested in parish renewal and at one stage I attended a weekend programme on this topic in Artane. Patrick McCabe played a major part and it seemed to me that he spoke very well and sincerely. He was well received. It is difficult to reconcile this with what we later learned about some of his activities.

From 1992 to 1995 I was chaplain to Cherry Orchard Hospital in west Dublin. At this time I began to be aware of the problem of child abuse. There were children in the hospital, many in single rooms because of their illnesses. As part of my work I used to go around the hospital to visit adults and children. I remember clearly that I wanted to bring a little cheer to the children during these visits. But no matter how good my intentions were, I would never know whether a particular child had been abused. A child's reaction could be simple shyness or it could be fear. Again, I am thankful that there was never a problem but I knew I had to be mindful of the possibility that a child had a history of which I knew nothing.

I have been horrified at the abuse which has taken place. How any human being comes to perpetrate such cruelty on a child is difficult to comprehend, even knowing some of the cruelty in our world. How a person who spends many years in training for the service of people in the ministerial priesthood can combine preaching the gospel with abuse of children seems unfathomable.

I have been shocked too at the failures to deal effectively and justly with allegations of abuse. Why this happened needed to be investigated. The Murphy Commission was established to investigate the handling of abuse by Church and state. I want this book to contribute to a better understanding of the whole topic.

2

The Impact of *The Murphy Report*

It was staggering. It seems impossible to exaggerate its impact. For a book that may not have reached the bestsellers' list, *The Murphy Report,* all 720 pages of it, was a roaring success. It seems odd to speak like this of a book about the awful reality of the sexual abuse of children but without a doubt it was the most talked-about and written-about book of 2009 in Ireland. In September 2013 an internet search on Google for '*Murphy Report* Dublin' yielded more than six million results.

I remember the day in November 2009 that this report on the handling of allegations of sexual abuse of children in the diocese of Dublin was published. Priests serving in the diocese had meetings some time beforehand to prepare for it but nothing could really have prepared us. I remember listening to the news bulletins, the interviews and the panel discussions. And the outrage – especially the outrage. It was like watching the twin towers of the World Trade Center collapsing in dust and rubble – and hundreds, if not thousands, of casualties. It was almost hypnotic, the devastation that *The Murphy Report* seemed to set loose on the world we knew.

I downloaded the report from the Department of Justice website and printed off the first parts of it to begin reading what it really said, behind what the media were reporting.

The following day came the tsunami – this time in the shape of the newspapers. Page after page of extracts and photographs of the 'villains' of the piece. The views of prominent journalists and other personalities. Wall to wall in the worst possible way. It was all-consuming. Remember seeing films of the Indian Ocean tsunami and the tsunami that affected the Fukushima nuclear power plant in Japan? Walls of water moving relentlessly on to the land and demolishing everything in their path? After the collapse of the towers, the news coverage in the days following *The Murphy Report* – no, not days, months – was like a tsunami completing the destruction. There was no escape, no relief.

Catholic bishops and other senior officials were shamed, by name, in public, by a government-appointed commission of investigation headed by a judge. They were not themselves accused of the sexual abuse of children and many of those who had abused were protected by pseudonyms. If anything it seemed worse for the bishops and diocesan officials: they were paraded in public as being the evil masterminds who enabled the abuse to continue, for their own selfish reasons. They sacrificed innocent children in order to preserve their own status and reputations and to protect the property of the Church. There had been scandal in 1992 when Bishop Éamon Casey was named as the father of a son and other scandals in the Church since then but they were as nothing compared to the reaction to *The Murphy Report*.

The tsunami was followed by something almost equally un-imaginable in Ireland: not one Catholic bishop or two but four sent in their resignations. The resignation of another was loudly and insistently demanded. A cardinal and a bishop were beyond the reach of demands for resignation, because they had already retired, but this did not mean that they were spared the outrage.

This may all sound over-dramatic and no, I'm not looking for sympathy. It cannot in any way be compared to what a sexually abused child goes through: the physical trauma; the total betrayal, often by a trusted adult; the emotional devastation; the burden of secrecy; being unable to confide in anyone; the sense of guilt, although completely unjustified; the hopelessness; the feeling of worthlessness and of abandonment.

Perhaps the greatest thing *The Murphy Report* has done is to give a voice to those who were abused. Although the task of the commission was to investigate how allegations were handled rather than the abuse itself, the report, in the process of its work, does tell stories of abuse. Various broadcast and print media had already given some coverage to the abused but the report brings a lot together and does so with an authoritative voice. This was widely welcomed.

It is hard to describe what it felt like to be a priest serving in the diocese of Dublin in November 2009, knowing that so many children had been abused, then badly let down by those to whom they turned for help, and knowing that the abuse had been inflicted by colleagues, trusted priests in the diocese. A few of them I knew, not well, but we were all part of the team. And the rest of us priests of the diocese were blackened by implication. We were told that we were part of a totally corrupt and evil organisation and even if we were not personally culpable, we were still responsible.

Strangely, it was a comfort to come to my parish church for Mass on the Sundays that followed and find people still there. There was the awful task of saying something about the report but the fact that people were there, perhaps saying little, just their presence, was a blessing in itself: to know that we were not cut off from the land of the living. There was support. They knew that not everybody was implicated. We survived and there was still everyday life and there was Christmas.

But from the start, I had a sense of unease, that something apart from the awful abuse and the disastrous handling was not right. There were things in the report that did not ring true. It took time and work to identify some of them. In those early days nobody wanted to hear this. Especially not the media. To raise any question about the report was to be accused of compounding the terrible injury done to those who had been abused, denying them both the validation of their stories and the closure of naming those who caused the injuries.

The report received almost total, uncritical acceptance in the media, despite the fact that some problematic issues were immediately obvious. This was the editorial of *The Irish Times* on 27 November 2009: 'Corruption of power and the fundamentally rotten nature of relations between the Catholic Church and the state has been laid bare in a damning report into the rape and sexual abuse of children in the Dublin archdiocese over a thirty-year period. Denial and cover-up was the order of the day…"Repulsive" is a word that comes to mind in considering the response by former Dublin bishops and archbishops to clerical child abuse…The vast majority of uninvolved priests turned a blind eye. As might be expected, given the traditional supine attitude of governments to the Catholic hierarchy, state agencies avoided involvement…It would be wrong to conclude that criminal behaviour by priests in the Dublin archdiocese was exceptional.'

On 3 December 2009 *An Phoblacht/Republican News* reported Sinn Féin Vice-President Mary Lou McDonald as saying: 'The report on clerical sexual abuse of children in Dublin exposes how the most powerful men in the Catholic Church in the Dublin diocese conspired to protect abusers of children. It was a gross betrayal of generations of children. It is especially damning that the state authorities facilitated the cover-up and allowed the Church to be beyond the reach of the law. Senior Gardaí, up to and including the level of commissioner, repeatedly turned a blind eye to crimes of clerical sexual abuse. Anyone, including Gardaí, found to be complicit in the cover-up of child abuse, must be arrested and made to face the full rigours of the law.'

An unsigned article in the *Irish Medical News* on 24 February 2010 commented: 'A little dust has already settled on *The Murphy Report* on clerical child sex abuse in the Dublin Archdiocese since it recently rocked the nation. The detail evident in *The Murphy Report* is truly damning. It amounts to a comprehensive indictment of the manner in which senior elements in the Catholic Church in Ireland stood pointedly and idly by, while a sizeable proportion of priests systematically abused children on a horrific scale. In this latest development, the mere naming of half a dozen bishops whose failure to act contributed to, protected and directly maintained an extraordinarily abusive system, is breathtaking arrogance.'

Criticism of the report was hard to find, except for some comments that it did not go far enough, that those named as culprits should face severe penalties. People expressed outrage that some bishops involved were still in office and demanded heads on plates. In the matter of sexual abuse of children, the worst possible allegation that could be made against someone is that they inflicted the abuse. Not far behind is 'cover-up' of abuse and protecting abusers. Not far behind that comes daring to challenge any part of *The Murphy Report*. After all what could possibly be wrong with it?

The Irish Times editorial quoted above mentions 'the traditional supine attitude'. Simply to accept the report without question is itself a manifestation of a supine attitude. A saying attributed to Edmund Burke (although also found elsewhere) is: 'To read without reflecting is like eating without digesting.' The widespread response to *The Murphy Report* has been to react without reflecting; to swallow without digesting. To date there has still been no critical examination of it.

I wrote an article about the report which was published in *The Furrow*, an Irish pastoral magazine, in February 2010, and which is reproduced in Appendix 4 of this book. I challenged *The Irish Times* and was eventually invited to write a 'Rite and Reason' column. I followed their specifications but the column was banned at the last minute. Eventually, after I had recourse to the press ombudsman, the newspaper agreed to publish it, in February 2010. Neither this nor the article in *The Furrow* received any publicity anywhere. I anticipate that any media coverage this book receives will be as nothing compared to the coverage given to the report on its original publication, or the publicity given to Chapter 20 on its publication in July 2013.

When it was originally published, some parts of *The Murphy Report* were omitted for legal reasons. Nearly four years after the initial publication, Chapter 20, the final part, was published in full. The time seems right for a more balanced assessment of the report.

This book does not in any way deny the reality or the horror of the abuse. It does not claim that all cases were handled well, nor that diocesan officials were beyond criticism in their handling of allegations. It attempts to examine the report in general and to focus specifically on Chapter 20 – the longest chapter and the last to be published – and the evidence it presents, as well as the assessments made by the commission of investigation. As far as possible, I offer facts to help in my analysis and I wish my book be judged on the truth or otherwise of its statements.

My purpose is not to declare that *The Murphy Report* is worthless. This is clearly not the case. Nor do I attempt to exonerate those with responsibility for handling the allegations of child abuse. I am in no position either to exonerate or to declare guilty. I am not here to defend bishops – I am often critical of their actions or lack of action – but they, like other human beings, deserve to be treated with truth and justice.

My proposition is that the evidence in the report itself, understood in the context of the times, makes a *prima facie* case for recognising that it is not a reliable means of assessing the culpability or otherwise of those named in the report who were responsible for the handling of allegations in the diocese.

If this is the case, a comprehensive evaluation of *The Murphy*

Report is required in order to serve the cause of justice. In order to do this, it will be necessary to find a way to lift the thirty-year embargo on the evidence put before the commission and to examine both the work of the commission and the legislation under which it was established.

In Chapter 10, I speculate about how the minds of members of the Murphy Commission may have worked towards producing the report but I do not question their motives. I have tried to state my own motives openly and clearly. I am very conscious of the horror of the abuse of children. The commission validates the stories of the abused and provides an authoritative public voice for their stories. The manner in which it interprets and assesses the handling of the abuse would appear at first to reinforce its service to those who were abused but when its interpretations and assessments show evidence of multiple errors, in reality it does a disservice to them. It is the Murphy Commission itself that damages its own credibility, when its interpretations and assessments are not substantiated by the evidence. This must not be taken as casting doubt on the stories of abuse which have been substantiated, nor as doubting the hurt caused through the processes of handling allegations of abuse. I believe we should hold strongly on to what is positive and valid in *The Murphy Report* while, in honesty and justice, dealing with its errors and failures.

I may be accused of trying to roll back the advances made by the report, which brought considerable comfort and closure to many who were abused by priests of the diocese of Dublin. I can only ask that what I write be assessed on the basis of the truth it reveals. If even some of what I write is true, errors in the report cannot be said to serve the cause of healing and justice. Let us not fear that truth will endanger truth.

I do not expect that everyone will agree with all I say in this book. I understand that some who read it may be upset or angry.

I am well aware that, like everyone else, I make mistakes, so if any reader finds errors of fact or faults in my reasoning, I will be glad to hear from them. All I ask is that my arguments themselves be addressed: personal attacks serve only to distract attention from the matter being discussed and hinder the process of justice for all concerned. The arguments I present will stand or fall on their own merits, whether readers are people of faith in God or not and whether they are lay people or are ordained for service in a church or religious body.

3

Revisiting *The Murphy Report*

Before proceeding, there is an important and complex question to be addressed. *The Murphy Report* has unusual status in Irish society. Not only is it seen as the ultimate answer on the issue of the handling of sexual abuse of children in the diocese of Dublin, it is promoted as a template for how commissions of investigation should be conducted.

The report presents many meticulously documented facts. These are not in question. The questions arise in regard to the interpretation and assessment of these facts. The report fails to address both the context of the times and the context of the pastoral mission of the Church.

Two possible extremes of responses to it might be:

1. *The Murphy Report* is the last word on the matter of sexual abuse of children in the diocese of Dublin, professionally carried out and virtually on a par with a supreme court ruling.
2. *The Murphy Report* is a disgrace, unfounded, a totally unwarranted attack on the Church.

I have heard much of the first reaction but I have never heard anything approaching the second. This book offers neither response. I accept that the commission accomplished much good work. This book points to clearly identifiable elements of the report, all of which I have evaluated on their own merits and which I invite readers to evaluate.

The commission of investigation worked for more than three

years, 2006-9; it had three members on its highly qualified legal team and ancillary staff to help it in its work. It processed a vast quantity of data in documents and witness interviews, much of which is now confidential. It was funded by the taxpayer. I have only my personal resources as a retired priest of the diocese of Dublin, my own limited experience and the data available to me in the public domain. If the well-resourced commission could fall into error, as I believe this book shows, it is not to be wondered at if I do the same. I trust that any reader who finds errors will not hesitate to enlighten me.

The Murphy Commission was not a court of law. The standard of proof in civil litigation is that a fact must be proven on the 'balance of probabilities', based on the evidence properly presented before the court. The standard applied in criminal cases is that the court must be satisfied of the defendant's guilt beyond reasonable doubt – a higher standard than that used in civil litigation.

A tribunal of enquiry is not a court of law; it is a process with accepted (potentially serious) consequences for all concerned. It is obliged to operate an appropriate standard of proof. The report of the Moriarty Tribunal (which investigated, from 1997, payments to certain politicians) puts it like this (1,60): '…it seemed to the tribunal that the adoption of a criminal standard of proof was neither warranted nor realistic; as indicated earlier in this chapter, the conclusions in a report such as this are in no sense findings of either criminal or civil liability in law and represent no more than what should be a reasoned and informed expression of opinion.'

If the standard of proof for a tribunal is no more than that it 'should be a reasoned and informed expression of opinion', this is at most the standard to which a commission of investigation would work. As a reasoned and informed expression of opinion, it clearly merits serious attention. It must not, however, be elevated to a quasi-unreformable status. We respect legal proceedings, while recognising that errors can be made. This is why we have courts of appeal. The findings of commissions of investigation deserve to be treated with respect but they do not have the same standing as the verdict of a court.

In paragraph 37 of her supreme court judgement on the Bovale case in 2011, Mrs Justice Susan Denham stated: '…the tribunal of enquiry is not imposing any liabilities or affecting any rights…its conclusions have merely the status of opinion…this opinion is devoid of legal consequences…its findings are sterile of legal effect…A tribunal of enquiry is a simple fact-finding-operation…The tribunal has no power to inflict a penalty and its determinations cannot form any basis for the punishment by any other authority of that person…'[*]

We know the judgements of lower courts can be appealed to a higher court, all the way to the supreme court. What about the supreme court itself? It would be exceptional for it to go back on a decision of its own but in the 1965 case of the Attorney General v. Ryan's Car Hire Ltd, the supreme court held that it may depart from an earlier decision for compelling reasons: 'Where a point has been entirely overlooked, or conceded without argument, the authority of the decision may be weakened to vanishing point.'[†]

This being the case, it would be entirely contrary to reason to say that the findings of a commission of investigation may not be revisited. In later pages of this book, I document points that the Murphy Commission entirely overlooked. Whether these were points conceded without argument in the processes of the commission I cannot say; if arguments took place, they rarely appear in the pages of the report.

---

[*]   Appeal No 25 and 26: Supreme Court Judgement 14/07/2011, p. 10, quoting J. Hardiman.

[†]   Quoted in Mary Redmond, 'Constitutional?', *The Furrow*, July-August, 2013, p. 396.

It seems quite clear that *The Murphy Report* can be revisited. This is particularly important in the light of Justice Denham's statement above: 'The tribunal has no power to inflict a penalty.' If this is true of a tribunal, it is surely just as valid in the case of a commission of investigation. If such a commission identifies individuals and assigns blame in a report that is published and receives extensive media attention, the commission in the very act of identifying and blaming inflicts a severe penalty.

Also of importance is Justice Denham's comment in relation to a tribunal: '…its conclusions have merely the status of opinion…' I do not recall anyone in the print or broadcast media making it clear in the months following the publication of *The Murphy Report* in November 2009 that its findings had 'merely the status of opinion'. The public perception was that the report was the definitive word. At the time a prominent journalist reprimanded me for questioning the report.

Some may assert that it is too late to revisit the report: that it is old news; that the public is no longer interested. It is possible to test this assertion. Others may wonder why I did not raise my concerns within months of the publication of the report? I tried to do so, in a limited way, but what is a lone voice against so many clamouring? Few listened. Few could imagine that anyone would dare to raise a voice. There was the sensitive matter of finding a way to be sure that questioning the report did not in any way diminish the horror of the abuse, or seem to ignore the catalogue of failures in dealing with allegations.

Questioning the report has taken time. The publication of Chapter 20 has provided the impetus. Even now, I am aware that there is much more to be done. I can only offer this book as a step in this direction.

'*Fiat justitia, ruat caelum*' is carved over the pillars on the Bridewell, at the Four Courts in Dublin: 'Let justice be done, even if the heavens be brought down!' A challenging motto, especially if doing justice means questioning the authorities of the state.

Readers may recall these words: 'This is such an appalling vista that every sensible person in the land would say that it cannot be right that these actions should go any further.' They were part of the judgement of Lord Justice Denning, then Master of the Rolls, on the appeal of the Birmingham Six in the British court of appeal in November 1979. He was contemplating the unimaginable scenario of the six men being successful. Their second full appeal, in 1991, was allowed.

Not that questioning the report has been described as an 'appalling vista' but sometimes the impression is given that any challenge to it will destroy everything that has been achieved. The report is not so precarious that this could happen. What is true in the report will stand by virtue of its truth.

4

The Opening Shot

Before addressing the content of Chapter 20, I would like to do what the Murphy Commission does: come out fighting. It fires a serious shot right at the start of its report, before it reveals any of the details of the abuse cases, calling into question the credibility and trustworthiness of the diocesan officials who had responsibility for dealing with allegations of child sexual abuse.

This is important. If the report can persuade readers at the beginning that diocesan officials were deceitful, untrustworthy, selfish and uncaring, this prepares the ground for them to be given more evidence to confirm this.

If we can show that the commission's judgement of diocesan officials is unwarranted by the evidence and that the diocese, like other organisations concerned with this terrible problem, was swamped by an unanticipated tsunami of allegations and cases and that, like state and professional bodies, it did not have the required knowledge and the essential understanding to respond effectively, subsequent evidence, as for example we will examine in Chapter 20 of the report, may be understood entirely differently.

Whether the commission was aware of what it was doing in the report, I cannot say. It may simply have seemed to them a logical way to proceed. But what the report does is what matters: it attacks the credibility of the officials of Dublin diocese, before adducing any evidence. Then the conclusions will follow naturally.

The opening paragraphs of Chapter 1, 'Overview', of *The Murphy Report,* 1.1 to 1.13, present background information: Introduction, *The Ryan Report,* 'The Number of Complaints' and

'The Priests – Where They Are Now'.

There follows immediately at 1.14 a section entitled 'The Archdiocese and Church Authorities'. This is the opening shot to which I refer. In the words of the report:

> The volume of revelations of child sexual abuse by clergy over the past 35 years or so has been described by a Church source as a 'tsunami' of sexual abuse. He went on to describe the 'tsunami' as 'an earthquake deep beneath the surface hidden from view'. The clear implication of that statement is that the Church, in common with the general public, was somehow taken by surprise by the volume of the revelations. Officials of the archdiocese of Dublin and other Church authorities have repeatedly claimed to have been, prior to the late 1990s, on 'a learning curve' in relation to the matter. Having completed its investigation, the commission does not accept the truth of such claims and assertions.

Despite the plausible language, the implications for the rest of the report are extremely serious. This is not polite, diplomatic language. This is blunt language. This is clear confrontation. The commission goes straight for the jugular.

What the commission is actually saying is this (please pardon my blunt translation):

Officials of the archdiocese of Dublin and other Church authorities have repeatedly claimed to have been, prior to the late 1990s, on 'a learning curve' in relation to the matter. Having completed its investigation over several years, the commission does not believe them. The commission believes that they were repeatedly telling lies. We, the commission, say very clearly that there was no such learning curve. The commission believes that we cannot trust what these people say.

They make another equally serious charge (again my words):

These people say that they were on a learning curve – that they did not have sufficient knowledge and understanding prior to the late 1990s. We do not believe them. We believe that they did have the requisite knowledge to deal effectively with the allegations of child sexual abuse and that they deliberately chose not to do so. They deliberately turned a blind eye and let children and families suffer.

The commission's words do not make these charges explicit but this is the clear meaning of what it is saying. Before it ever gets into the subject matter proper, it makes this categorical judgement that would, if verified, cut the ground from under anything that Church officials would say or do. Look now at the first part of the paragraph, in which the commission also rejects the diocese's version of events (these are the words of the report):

> The volume of revelations of child sexual abuse by clergy over the past 35 years or so has been described by a Church source as a 'tsunami' of sexual abuse. He went on to describe the 'tsunami' as 'an earthquake deep beneath the surface hidden from view'. The clear implication of that statement is that the Church, in common with the general public, was somehow taken by surprise by the volume of the revelations.

The Church source referred to here is not one of the officials with diocesan responsibility in the matter of child sexual abuse allegations. In a footnote he is identified as A. McGrady, a member of the staff of Mater Dei Institute, a diocesan foundation. The commission misquotes Mr McGrady, who did not describe a tsunami as 'an earthquake deep beneath the surface'. He wrote: 'Sex abuse has hit the Irish church like a tsunami. The earthquake at its source was largely unwitnessed, it took place deep below the surface...'

In rejecting his description and in the implication that the Church was not in reality taken by surprise by the volume of the revelations, the commission is saying very clearly (in my translation of what their words mean): They were not taken by surprise. They knew all along. They have no excuse.

I do not know whether this tone was used in the interviews at the sessions of the commission. I do know that the report tells the diocesan officials and the country: 'We do not accept that you are telling the truth. We do not trust what you tell us.'

It is understandable that the members of the commission would feel great anger and disgust at the accounts of abuse which were under their gaze for the three years they sat, all the more so as we have come to understand the drastic and lasting effect that abuse can have on a person who has been abused. This anger and disgust would have been shared by the vast majority of people in the country, as they too came to understand the effects. I have no doubt that the anger and disgust were shared by the diocesan officials as they too came to understand it. Is it possible that the commission transferred its anger and disgust to the officials of the diocese in such a way that the misplaced anger appears to cloud their interpretations of evidence and their assessments? If so, this gives deep cause for concern.

When the commission goes beyond the investigation of how diocesan and state officials struggled to deal with difficult situations with limited knowledge and resources and assigns blame for failure in those situations, it begins to act in a quasi-judicial manner. It is all the more serious when the commission accuses the officials of acting from base motives.

Of course the diocesan and state officials made mistakes. Nobody had the 'solution' to child sexual abuse then. Even now, nobody has the solution, despite all the study and work that have been done over the past twenty or thirty years. All we have even today are ways to contain and to some extent manage the abuse, the abusers and the consequences. When officials with responsibility for dealing with instances of child sexual abuse over twenty or thirty years and who experienced little success and much failure in the attempt are judged culpable by a commission whose members show no understanding of the conditions of the time and who fail to place the issue in the context of how frequent such abuse is in Irish society, it appears that anything these officials did, even applying the very best knowledge of the time, may be used against them.

In order to establish the validity of its rejection of the claims of diocesan officials, the commission needs to have a watertight case. Let us examine the three assertions the commission makes about diocesan officials:

1. They cannot use the excuse that they were taken by surprise by a 'tsunami'.
2. There was no learning curve – they were well enough aware from the start.
3. We cannot trust what these people say or even say repeatedly.

1. Was there a tsunami of cases which took the diocese by surprise?

The commission seems to ignore the statistics of complaints to the diocese they themselves document in 1.19:

	Complaints	Suspicions	Totals
1960s	3	0	3
1970s	11	2	13
1980s	64	24	88
1990s	135	23	158
Increase	x 45		x 52.61

If this is not a transition from a relatively calm sea to a catastrophe, I do not know what the commission understands by a tsunami. To say that church officials were 'somehow taken by surprise by the volume of the revelations' is putting it very mildly indeed. The 'Church source' gave a very good description of the impact.

A similar surge in cases is reported on p. 23 of *Child Protection Practices in Ireland: A Case Study*. Nationally, the number of child abuse referrals to health boards rose between 1983 and 1995, with the increase in notifications of sexual abuse far greater than that for abuse in general:

	1983	1995	Increase
Child abuse notifications	434	6,415	x 14.78
Child sexual abuse	37	2,441	x 65.97

This tsunami of cases is reflected in statistics from the Dublin Rape Crisis Centre (DRCC) and the Eastern Health Board of the time. If the Murphy Commission were to refuse to believe that the health boards and the DRCC were also 'somehow taken by surprise by the volume of the revelations', the absurdity of such a statement would be obvious.

In the Department of Health's *Memorandum on Non-Accidental Injuries to Children* (March 1977) the word 'sexual' is never used. This was the handbook for the doctors who were directors of community care in the eight health boards and twenty-six community care areas around the country. Revisions of these guidelines in 1980 and 1983 continued to deal only with physical abuse and neglect. It was not until a further revision in 1987 that sexual abuse was recognised as a distinct category. Even then the Department of Health's *Child Abuse Guidelines* stated: 'The procedures to be followed in dealing with child sexual abuse do not differ from the general guidelines. However, the identification and validation of child sexual abuse is fundamentally different.' So there was much further to go. If Dublin diocesan officials were somewhat ahead of state authorities in beginning to grapple with the tsunami of child sexual abuse, this, despite all their failures, is surely reason for praise rather than for blame.

This is similar to the development of understanding in the UK. Jane Wynne reports in *Creative Responses to Child Sexual Abuse* (Richardson and Bacon eds., 2003): 'Child sexual abuse was not recognised as a category of abuse on child protection registers until 1986 and no official advice was available from the Department of Health (DH) or professional bodies until after the Cleveland crisis in 1987…1991: Publication of first Royal College of Physicians (RCP) report on physical signs in child sexual abuse.' (p. 101)

'…At Easter 1987 there was an embargo on child abuse papers at the annual meeting of the BPA (British Paediatric Association). Child sexual abuse, a subject in which we were all on a steep learning curve, was not open for formal discussion by the profession's leading organisation.' (p. 103.)

Was there a learning curve, or were officials well enough aware from the start?

From the early centuries of its existence, the Church understood sexual abuse of children as clearly wrong but to say that church officials knew about what today we call child sexual abuse and knew that it was wrong cannot be taken to mean that diocesan officials in Dublin in the 1970s and 1980s understood what came to be known in the late 1990s. This is an area of study that has developed only over the past forty years. By the late 1990s diocesan officials had a reasonable grasp of the situation, or they would not have been able to produce the *Framework Document* in 1996 to guide the handling of cases.

Other evidence is available of the very recent nature of this understanding. The Church of Ireland [Anglican Communion] issued its first guidelines in 1997: *Safeguarding Trust: The Church of Ireland Code of Good Practice for Ministry with Children.* It issued a fourth edition in 2008. The Presbyterian Church in Ireland issued the fourth edition of its guidelines, *Taking Care Two*, in 2011. In 1995 the Methodist Church in Ireland put together its first child protection policy document, *Keep Them Safe*.

The unspoken implication of the commission's denying the learning curve is that they considered that diocesan officials had substantially this level both of knowledge and of understanding at the beginning of the period which the commission was investigating, 1975. Diocesan officials had some knowledge in the 1970s but could they have had the kind of understanding that Irish society was arriving at in the late 1990s? There are many dimensions to this question:

• Learning the extent of the abuse.
• Learning to understand the gravity of the effects of child sexual abuse on the child and, as the years pass, the effects on the adult who was abused as a child.
• Learning to understand the mentality and modes of operation of a person who sexually abuses a child and his or her motivation and deviousness in the process.
• Learning to devise the best way of assessing offenders, understanding the likelihood or not of the person re-offending whether with or without treatment and devising and implementing the best methods of treatment and the most effective ways of monitoring the offender afterwards.
• The process of development of effective procedures and getting a variety of agencies to communicate and work effectively together on the matter.
• Legal processes.

It can be difficult to prove a negative. How could the diocesan officials who were so criticised by the commission possibly prove that they did not have all this knowledge and understanding in the 1970s? There are two ways of dealing with this: to prove that, whatever knowledge they had, they could not have had the knowledge and understanding that came twenty or more years later; and to show that arguments by the commission that they had this knowledge do not stand up to scrutiny.

I believe it is possible to prove that Dublin diocesan officials could not have had the required knowledge. To prove that there was no 'learning curve', as claimed repeatedly by bishops and officials of Dublin diocese and by other Church authorities, *The Murphy Report* would have to prove that they had substantially the same level of knowledge and understanding in the 1970s, in the 1980s and in the first half of the 1990s as they had in 1996, when the *Framework Document* was published. There is no proof of this in the report; just the blunt assertion at 1.14: 'Having completed its investigation, the commission does not accept the truth of such claims and assertions.'

Up to the 1990s, if I heard about child abuse, I would have thought of physical or emotional abuse or neglect. I never dreamed that sexual abuse of children happened. Call me naïve but that was the case. It was never mentioned in my seven years of preparation for ordination in 1967. *The Murphy Report* (10.19) states: '…in the years 1970-95, there was no structured training on matters concerning child sexual abuse by priests or others.' Those who trained us at the time were in the same position. It simply was not a public issue. While it was a tragic part of the experience of those who were abused, it remained firmly below the radar.

I also offer two indications of the state of knowledge in North America, where the phenomenon of child sexual abuse first began to be the object of serious concern and study:

Firstly the Canadian publication, 'A Meta-analysis of the Published Research on the Effects of Child Sexual Abuse' analyses thirty-seven studies published between 1981 and 1995, twenty-two of them in US. Note that the earliest study included here is from 1981. Secondly, as recently as 2004, Professor B.J. Cling of John Jay College of Criminal Justice (New York) writes in *Sexualized Violence Against Women and Children*:

'It is time and well past time, to integrate child abuse and trauma studies into mainstream university curricula and professional training programs. The issues are central, not peripheral.

'By the early 21st century, the issue of child sexual abuse has become a legitimate focus of professional attention, while increasingly separated from second wave feminism*...As child sexual abuse becomes absorbed into the larger field of interpersonal trauma studies, child sexual abuse studies and intervention strategies have become degendered and largely unaware of their political origins in modern feminism and other vibrant political movements of the 1970s. One may hope that unlike in the past, this rediscovery of child sexual abuse that began in the 70s will not again be followed by collective amnesia...To the extent that the second wave of feminism, at least in academic settings, has become fragmented, preoccupied with identity politics and theory and marginalized, there exists a danger that public policy attention to child sexual abuse prevention, evaluation and treatment may correspondingly fragment and weaken in the early 21st century.'

The very first sentence of this extract from Professor Cling is telling: in 2004, he sees it as 'well past time' to integrate studies on child abuse into academic and professional training, something that, clearly, had not been done in the United States. What about Ireland in the 1970s or earlier? Is there any such programme in Ireland even now? Did the commission investigate how many, if any, psychiatrists or lawyers or social workers in Ireland in the 1970s, 1980s or 1990s had taken part in such a programme? Did

---

* Second-wave feminism was the feminist movement from the 1960s to about 1990, as distinguished from first-wave feminism of the late 1800s and the early 1900s, which included the suffrage movement.

they investigate how many priests or bishops had done so?

Further evidence can be drawn from statistics of the Dublin Rape Crisis Centre, which was established in 1979. Annual reports from the Centre for 2005 and 2012 show the current level of the profile of child sexual abuse:

	2012	2005
Adult rape	44.21%	45.2%
Child sexual abuse	42.04%	45.7%
Adult sexual assault	8,41%	6%

But earlier statistics from an Eastern Health Board report on the Rape Crisis Centre (*The Dublin Rape Crisis Centre: A Process Evaluation*, October 1989) show the huge change 1980-6:

	1980	1986
Rape and attempted rape	88%	29%
Child sexual abuse	0%	67%

The report comments: 'The 1983 report contains the first documented reference indicating that the centre was beginning to provide services to a significant number of girls who are/were victims of incest. From the 1984 report it is clear that this trend has become firmly established with over one third of the total number of cases dealt with relating to what is described as 'child sexual abuse'. (p. 7)

'The figures clearly indicate the growing number of child sexual abuse cases contacting the RCC. In 1980 11 per cent of clients were aged fifteen or under at the time of assault/abuse whereas, by 1988, 66 per cent of clients were aged fifteen or under.' (p. 25)

This is a remarkable change between the years 1980 and 1986. This is not to say that no abuse was taking place in 1980 but it does mean that it was not publicly addressed. Clearly the need for services dealing with child sexual abuse had just begun to be evident in the early 1980s.

This is confirmed by records of the number of new cases of alleged and confirmed child abuse in Ireland and in the Eastern Health Board Region over just four years 1984-7, as reported in *The Economic and Social Review* of January 1991. They distinguish the numbers of cases referred and the numbers of cases confirmed as CSA (child sexual abuse):

New Cases of Alleged and Confirmed Child Abuse in Ireland

	1984	1985	1986	1987	Factor increase 1984-7
All child abuse referrals	479	767	1,015	1,646	x3.4
CSA referrals	88	234	475	929	x10.7
CSA as % of all referrals	18.4	30.5	46.8	56.4	x3.1
All confirmed child abuse	182	304	495	763	x4.2
CSA confirmed	33	133	274	456	x13.8
CSA confirmed as % of all confirmed	18.1	43.8	55.4	59.8	

New Cases of Alleged and Confirmed Child Abuse in EHB Region

	1984	1985	1986	1987	Factor increase 1984-7
CSA confirmed	11	42	134	211	x19.2

An increase by a factor of 13.8 in confirmed CSA cases for Ireland and by a factor of 19.2 for the EHB region over a period of four years certainly looks like a totally unanticipated tsunami. *The Murphy Report* does not provide any comparison between how health authorities coped with this increase and how the diocese of Dublin coped with its tsunami. Nor does it tell us whether the health authorities reported all these cases to the Gardaí.

This was just the beginning of the realisation of the extent of the problem. Understanding the depth of the injury and its long-lasting effects and finding any way of dealing with abusers had still to come. If this was the reality for the RCC, which was not established to deal with sexual abuse of children but with the rape of adults, how can the commission possibly say that diocesan officials were bluffing when they said that they did not know the extent of the problem or how to deal with it?

The commission appears not be aware of the following comment in *The Ferns Report* (pp. 11-12):

'In May 1975 an expert group was brought together by the Department of Health to establish the extent of the problem of non-accidental injuries to children...In March 1976, the expert group published a report on non-accidental injury to children and this led to the 1977 *Memorandum on Non-Accidental Injury to Children* issued by the Department of Health. This memorandum and the report leading up to it, made no reference to the sexual abuse of children. Further guidelines published in 1983 mentioned sexual abuse of children in passing but it was not until 1987 that the Department of Health child abuse guidelines set out procedures for the identification, investigation and management of child sexual abuse...All of these guidelines dealt with child abuse perpetrated by a member of the family or the carer of the child and did not advert in any detail to the situation of the child being abused by third parties...These guidelines did not address the issue of allegations of child sexual abuse which were not reported until the victim had become an adult...It is generally accepted that awareness of the nature of child sexual abuse in Ireland coincided with high profile cases such as the Kilkenny Incest Investigation in 1993 and the west of

Ireland farmer case in 1995.'

Speaking during a Dáil debate on the Kilkenny Incest Investigation on 3 March 1993, the Minister for Health, Brendan Howlin said: 'The terrifying sexual abuse suffered as a child by the young woman happened at a time when the existence of child sexual abuse was not even publicly acknowledged. For example, the taskforce on childcare services which reported in 1980 made scant reference to the incidence of incest and other forms of sexual abuse against vulnerable children. This taskforce was composed of a number of experts in childcare and its report focused on what were the major issues of the time. I make this point not in any way to denigrate the excellent work undertaken by that taskforce but to illustrate the lack of awareness of child sexual abuse at the time.'

Is *The Ferns Report* correct when it states that 'awareness of the nature of child sexual abuse in Ireland' came in the 1990s? How is it possible for the Murphy Commission so to denigrate the best efforts of diocesan officials in times when, according to the then Minister for Health, 'the existence of child sexual abuse was not even publicly acknowledged'?

Further confirmation of how little diocesan officials suspected the extent of the problem is found in Chapter 20 of *The Murphy Report* itself, at 20.100: 'An insurance policy was issued in March 1987':

> The initial premium was £515, with a limit on any single claim of £50,000. There was a stated limit of aggregate cover of £200,000 for all claims during the period of cover. The first period of cover was between 2 March 1987 and 1 March 1988. The then general insurance manager in Church and General told the commission that he did not believe that he would have offered this type of cover to the general market at the time. (9.6)[*]

---

[*] Average weekly wages in 1987 convert to €307 in the industrial sector and €471 in public, administrative and defence: www.esri.ie/pdf/QEC0404_Casey.pdf, p. 16.

The report concludes:

The taking out of insurance was an act proving knowledge of child sexual abuse as a potential major cost to the archdiocese and is inconsistent with the view that Archdiocesan officials were still 'on a learning curve' at a much later date, or were lacking in an appreciation of the phenomenon of clerical child sex abuse. (1.21)

But with the benefit of hindsight it is clear that the derisory premium and insured sum in such a serious matter are an indication that neither the archbishop nor the insurance company, with all its business experience, had any realistic understanding of how serious the whole issue would be.

During this period, how aware were our reporters and journalists of sexual abuse? An online archive search of *The Irish Times* from 1859 reveals that the first time the word 'paedophile' was used in the newspaper was in an article by Maeve Binchy on 12 August 1975. Then the increase: 1975-95 – 477 hits: about 23 per year; 1996 to 29 March 2012 – 2030 hits: about 127 per year. The earliest reference I can find to sexual abuse of children occurs on 25 February 1971.

In relation to this, the arguments of the commission do not stand up to scrutiny. The diocesan officials could have had limited knowledge that some people sexually abuse children but it was simply impossible for them to have had the kind of understanding of the nature of the abuse, the effects on the abused person and the difficulties of dealing with the abuser that they were beginning to acquire by the late 1990s.

Indeed, religious authorities and state authorities and the relevant professions are still on a learning curve and are likely to be on it for a considerable length of time. We do not have good records of how the Garda has handled allegations of child sexual abuse but they, like other police forces around the world, have been on a steep learning curve over the past thirty years in their handling of allegations of rape. The 2nd edition of their *Recent Rape/Sexual Assault: National Guidelines on Referral and Forensic Clinical Examination in Ireland* is dated 2010. In addition, the Garda Inspectorate published *Responding to Child Sexual Abuse* in 2012. This includes one chapter dealing with Garda handling of the cases covered by *The Murphy Report*. The *Children First* document of 2011 from the Department of Children and Youth Affairs updates guidance for HSE Children and Family Services.

Knowing that this is the case, we can see the arguments of the commission in quite a different light. It will be sufficient to take one such argument, about Archbishop Ryan, from Chapter 20 of *The Murphy Report*, as an example.

The report (20.26-28) states:

> However, a memo written by Archbishop Ryan in 1981 states that, at the time of this [Artane] appointment, he "spoke to Father McCabe reminding him of the seriousness of his actions and the risk that he ran of imprisonment, quite apart from the scandal that had arisen and the even more public scandal that could arise in the future…"This memo indicates that Archbishop Ryan had a fuller understanding of the nature and extent of Father McCabe's problems than other documents might suggest.

This seems like an attempt by the commission to bolster their assertion that there was no learning curve. The report returns to a similar approach in 20.36, again referring to 1981:

> Archbishop Ryan was fully aware, at that time, of the criminal nature of Father McCabe's misconduct and, further, he was aware that such misconduct was damaging to children. He summarised the damage done as follows:
> '1. The most distressing feature of Father McCabe's failures is

the effect they are likely to have on the young people involved. Apparently their ages range, in so far as I know, from 6-16…'

There is no documentation whatsoever here, or anywhere else in the report that I can find, that even suggests that Archbishop Ryan or any other person could have had the same kind of understanding in 1981 that was arrived at in the late 1990s.

Again, the simplistic statement in 20.176: '[Archbishop Ryan] had a considerable understanding of the effects of abuse on children' seems aimed at dismissing, as at 1.14 of the report, any possibility that he and other diocesan authorities were on a 'learning curve'. He certainly had some knowledge for the time and perhaps more than some but it is overwhelmingly obvious that this was nothing like the knowledge we have today.

This is seen in *The Murphy Report* itself, in its account in Chapter 6 (beginning at 6.37) of the development of child protection services in the state. Two particularly important paragraphs:

Social workers told the commission that awareness and knowledge of child sexual abuse did not emerge in Ireland until about the early 1980s. The HSE told the commission that 'In the mid-1970s there was no public, professional or Government perception either in Ireland or internationally that child sexual abuse constituted a societal problem or was a major risk to children. (6.53)

In 1982, some social workers from the EHB area visited California to work with people dealing with sexual abuse there. In 1983 the Irish Association of Social Workers held a conference on child sexual abuse in Dublin. In 1988, child sexual abuse assessment units were established in Our Lady's Hospital for Sick Children, Crumlin (the St Louise Unit) and in Children's University Hospital, Temple Street (the St Claire's Unit). (6.54)

Note that it was also in 1988 that Father Patrick McCabe was laicised, following many interventions since the first complaint about him in 1977. It is to the credit of Archbishop Ryan that he was so farseeing at the time in his dealings with the case, even though in the end it all proved futile. But to use this as a stick with which to beat him, or to attribute to him then the kind of understanding that was only being arrived at in the late 1990s, is quite irrational.

2.   Can we trust what these people say, even say repeatedly?

All the above information is clear evidence that the commission seriously erred in not trusting what the officials of the diocese told them repeatedly.

There is no indication in *The Murphy Report* that the commission takes account of the late developments of awareness of child sexual abuse. We must assume that the commission did not know about this. If the Rape Crisis Centre itself was on such a steep learning curve, it would of necessity be later again before their work became part of public awareness. In 1979, when the centre started, even adult rape was a taboo subject and the centre faced considerable opposition. As for sexual abuse of children, when this began to be spoken of, there was reluctance to admit that it happened in Ireland. Nobody knew about it – except, of course, those who were abused (and their abusers).

If further evidence of the lack of understanding among state authorities and in the Murphy Commission were needed, we see it in the dealings of the commission with the HSE (6.59-6.67). The report states in relation to its dealings in 2006:

> On 27 October, the commission told the HSE that it was willing to further delay the issuing of an order for discovery provided substantive proposals including a time scale for the delivery of documents were put before the commission by 3 November 2006. The HSE informed the commission on 3 November 2006 that there

were 114,000 social work files covering the period of the commission's remit and that these were in up to fifty different locations. It was estimated that it would take half a day to read and consider each file. The commission concluded that it would take nearly ten years to complete this process. (6.62)

The commission was hopelessly optimistic in its estimate of 'nearly ten years'. If 114,000 social work files would take an average of half a day each to read and consider, it would take 57,000 workdays to complete the task. Working fifty-two weeks a year full-time for five days per week, doing nothing else, it would have taken an extra twenty-two full-time staff without holidays or sick leave to complete the task in ten years. And how long would it take to make something useful out of all this information? Paragraph 2.19 gives the number as 180,000 HSE files and still estimates only ten years!

The commission had complained in Chapter 2 of the volume of work involved in processing just the diocesan files:

The discovery process was protracted by a number of factors. In the case of the Dublin Archdiocese, the sheer volume of material to be discovered – over 70,000 documents – was hugely time-consuming. The commission was fortunate in that the archdiocese had assembled a good deal of its documentation in connection with a Garda investigation that took place subsequent to the Prime Time programme *Cardinal Secrets* which was broadcast in 2002 (see Chapter 5). The Archdiocese had transferred that information onto a computer program, much of which was transferred to the commission. (2.18)

This comment illustrates how unrealistic the commission's understanding and expectations were. If the diocesan documents had not been so well kept and so accessible, one wonders whether the Murphy Commission could ever have produced a report. Garda documentation 'was quite extensive for the period after 1995' (2.20). As it is, the fact that the bulk of the documents examined came from the diocese rather than from the state means that the commission's attention was focused far more on diocesan handling of abuse allegations than on their handling by state authorities. The state was largely off the hook.

This also makes it very difficult for us to understand how the commission can be so dismissive and condemnatory of diocesan administration in the matter of allegations of child sexual abuse. If, in the view of the commission, the diocese manages matters badly, it is reason for condemnation. If, in the view of the commission, the diocese manages matters well (although with little success in the end), it is also reason for condemnation. Of course mistakes were made in situations that had never been experienced before. But for the commission, failure is reason for assigning blame, even when success was beyond reach.

Chapter 20 and the report as a whole show little understanding by the commission of the importance of historical context. If the commission is to assess and criticise the actions of Church and state authorities over the period 1975-2004, it simply cannot do this unless it first establishes what the general state of knowledge was at different phases throughout this period and what would have been regarded as best practice in those times for dealing with child sexual abuse and abusers – if indeed there were any such things as 'best practice' guidelines at the time. It would also need to establish the prevalence of child sexual abuse in Irish society, in order to put abuse by priests in context. This is not a matter of excusing the inexcusable but of understanding reality.

When I was at school, corporal punishment was seen as 'best practice'. Many people thought schools could not function without it. Industrial schools and reformatories, when originally established, were not 'care homes' as we would expect today: they were part of the penal system. Those committed to them were not seen so much as unfortunate children in need of love and attention but as a problem, even a danger, to respectable society and requiring harsh discipline to make them reform and become industrious citizens. This was generally accepted by society.

This is not to assert that all was well. Some of the people who administered the system were guilty of cruelty. But it is an injustice to condemn, by today's standards, all those involved, including those groups or religious congregations who put their own resources at the service of the state. It is similarly an injustice to reject, despite much evidence to the contrary, even within *The Murphy Report*, the claim by diocesan authorities to have been, prior to the late 1990s, on 'a learning curve' in relation to the matter.

Remembering is a very important aspect of human life but it can sometimes be dangerous. We may forget what life was really like back then and presume that it was as we know it to be today. Most Irish people over about thirty-five, especially men, will remember a time when corporal punishment was generally accepted in schools. Younger people may find this hard to believe. It does not mean that schools then were run by evil and violent people. Some were violent; most were people who lived according to the accepted wisdom of the time.

In recent years, there has been such a torrent of debate about child sexual abuse in the media that we may presume too easily that it has always been like this. Think back to April 2002, when the *Sexual Abuse and Violence in Ireland (SAVI)* survey was published. This was a very thorough survey carried out by the Royal College of Surgeons for the Rape Crisis Centre. The *SAVI* report is arguably far more significant than any of the Church reports but the only reference I can find to it in *The Murphy Report* is in the bibliography (p. 679). Ask your friends if they remember the *SAVI* report. I have asked people and very few have a recollection of it. There was no public outrage when it came out; media reporting was minimal. This tells us a lot about public awareness. It was as recent as 2002.

The Czech writer Milan Kundera was a communist in the early days of communist rule in Czechoslovakia and in his idealism he reported a spy to the secret police on one occasion in 1950. This was before communist rule there developed into the totalitarianism for which the period is remembered. Kundera wrote in Chapter 8 of *Testaments Betrayed* (1993):

'Knowing neither the meaning nor the future course of history, knowing not even the objective meaning of their own actions (by which they 'involuntarily' participate in events whose meaning is 'concealed from them'), they proceed through their lives as one proceeds in the fog. I say fog, not darkness. In the darkness, we see nothing, we are blind, we are defenceless, we are not free. In the fog, we are free but it is the freedom of a person in fog: he sees fifty yards ahead of him, he can clearly make out the features of his interlocutor, can take pleasure in the beauty of the trees that line the path and can even observe what is happening close by and react.

'Man proceeds in the fog. But when he looks back to judge people of the past, he sees no fog on their path. From his present, which was their faraway future, their path looks perfectly clear to him, good visibility all the way. Looking back, he sees the path, he sees the people proceeding, he sees their mistakes but not the fog. And yet all of them – Heidegger, Mayakovsky*, Aragon, Ezra Pound, Gorky, Gottfried Benn, St John Perse, Giono – all were walking in fog and one might wonder: who is more blind? Mayakovsky, who as he wrote his poem on Lenin did not know where Leninism would lead? Or we, who judge him decades later and do not see the fog that enveloped him?

---

* Vladimir Mayakovsky (1893-1930) was a Russian poet who became disillusioned with the course the Soviet Union was taking

'Mayakovsky's blindness is part of the eternal human condition.

'But for us not to see the fog on Mayakovsky's path is to forget what man is, forget what we ourselves are.'

In another thirty or forty years, people may look back at what we, with the very best of intentions and with the best knowledge available to us, are doing about child sexual abuse and other serious wrongs in society. Will they judge us as clearly ill-intentioned, or will they see the fog in which we live, of which we are not aware?

If, with the benefit of hindsight, we judge the actions of those who did not have the benefit of the knowledge we have today and if we fail to acknowledge the 'fog' in their lives, we do worse than condemn them. We deny the blindness which is part of the eternal human condition, including ours. We forget what we ourselves are. By doing this, we serve neither truth nor justice.

When the Murphy Commission prefaces its rejection of the learning curve by the phrase 'having completed its investigation', it implies that it has investigated the claim that there was a learning curve. Whatever investigation it carried out, it fell far short of what is required for the very serious task that was its mandate. It clearly did not carry out even an elementary investigation of the textbooks used for the training of priests before the year 2000, to find out whether the matter of sexual abuse of children was covered. Neither, it would appear, did it check in the fields of medicine and social work, nor did the members even recall whether it was covered in their own training in law. Various accounts and revelations, such as those relating to Jimmy Savile, who died in October 2011, show that organisations other than the Catholic Church continued to fail to deal effectively with allegations of child sexual abuse, even after much improved knowledge and understanding became available and long after the Catholic Church in Ireland introduced safeguards, beginning with its *Framework Document* of 1996.

The terms of reference for *The Ferns Enquiry* of 2005 stated clearly, twice, that the task of the enquiry was to consider matters 'in the context of the time' (emphasis mine):

A. To consider whether the response was adequate or appropriate, *judged in the context of the time when the complaint or allegation was made* and if the response to the complaint or allegation appears inadequate or inappropriate when judged by those standards, to identify if possible the reason or reasons for this and report thereon.

B. To consider the response of diocesan and other Church authorities and the state authorities to cases where they had knowledge or strong and clear suspicion of sexual abuse involving priests of the Diocese of Ferns and to consider whether that response was adequate or appropriate *judged in the context of the time when the knowledge was acquired or the suspicion formed.*

This element was not included in the terms of reference of the Murphy Commission but this does not mean that the commission could safely ignore it. It should have been clear to commission members that they could not fulfil their mandate without keeping the 'context of the time' always in mind.

One might say: 'Well, those people in the Church didn't know but they should have known! It was their job, their responsibility!' That sounds reasonable but it is futile. It would be like saying: 'They should have had antibiotics in the 1918 flu pandemic which took somewhere between twenty-five million and a hundred million lives!' Yes, a great tragedy. But they didn't have antibiotics. No one knew anything about antibiotics at that time. It was not until 1928 that Alexander Fleming discovered penicillin.

Another example of the report being out of touch with reality in relation to the development of knowledge and understanding is found at 1.113: 'The welfare of children, which should have been the first priority, was not even a factor to be considered in the early stages.'

When I was in primary and secondary school in Dublin in the 1940s and 1950s, there was no such thing as a special needs assistant, although there must have been children who were dyslexic or autistic. By the standards of *The Murphy Report,* one might accuse teachers then of not having the welfare of children as a priority. The reality is much simpler: the welfare of children was provided for according to the understanding of the time. The sexual abuse of children was not considered a distinct category of abuse by Department of Health guidelines until 1987.

The point is well expressed by the *Onderzoekscommissie,* the commission on child sexual abuse in the Catholic Church in the Netherlands. The summary report in English supplied by the commission in December 2011 states its approach on p. 1: 'The commission of enquiry based its findings on empirical data from the reports of sexual abuse it received between March and December 2010, as well as historical records from ecclesiastical and other archives. It reviewed this information in light of the social, cultural, economic and political developments that have occurred over the last sixty-five years in the Netherlands and in the Roman Catholic Church. For the purposes of the study, a proper understanding of those changes was required to place the findings regarding the occurrence and explanation of the sexual abuse in its proper context. This should not, however, be taken to imply that a description of the sociocultural and historic context legitimises abuses.'

Although the understanding of the sociocultural and historical context cannot legitimise abuses it can help us understand the situation and the difficulties faced by those responsible for dealing with allegations of abuse and their very limited understanding

The report from the Netherlands also comments (p. 11): '... the impression that sexual abuse of minors occurred primarily within the Roman Catholic Church needs to be qualified. Sexual abuse of minors occurs widely in Dutch society.' The *SAVI* report of 2002 comes to a similar conclusion.

But *The Murphy Report* does more than just ignore reality. It goes a giant step further. In its opening argument, it inexplicably denies reality. It is so audacious as to state categorically (the words are mine): 'These people, who were dealing with rapidly increasing numbers of allegations of child sexual abuse for more than twenty years up to the late 1990s, were certainly not on the learning curve they claim in this matter. The commission does not accept the truth of such claims and assertions! These people are not to be trusted!'

Perhaps because this claim is so categorical and seems to offer a plain and simple truth, a clear explanation, along with naming guilty parties, the public and media were led, quite contrary to common sense, to accept it. Most extraordinary of all, some church leaders and officials were themselves induced to doubt their own experience and accept the narrative laid down by the commission. Those who realised how badly the commission had erred seem to have been reduced to silence. To dare to dissent was to be shouted down and to be condemned further.

It would be a mistake to accept the assessment so categorically given by the Murphy Commission in regard to the learning curve, since its foundation is not on rock but on quicksand. In claiming the moral high ground right at the start (1.14), the commission does not cut the ground from under the feet of the Church officials. This is how the report begins its argument in its first chapter, with the rejection of the 'learning curve' claim. The report is just as absolute when it states (1.113):

The commission has no doubt that clerical child sexual abuse was covered up by the archdiocese of Dublin and other Church authorities over much of the period covered by the commission's remit.

'Cover-up' is a fact of human life. We have ample evidence of it in our world today with whistle blowers and Wikileaks. But if the bishops and other diocesan officials, while having some limited knowledge, did not have the level of knowledge and understanding required to address the problem of clerical sexual abuse of children, it seems clear that they cannot be accused of covering up as they are accused in the report. They undoubtedly made mistakes in trying to deal with a difficult situation – diocesan officials are as human as the members of the Murphy Commission. There was a concern for confidentiality in this sensitive matter; if there were not, it would be cause for blame. There were no 'designated' people or well-developed procedures, so by today's standards the handling of allegations was seriously defective. There was concern for the reputation of the Church, as there would be in any organisation. There was concern for the assets of the Church – there had to be, if the Church were to continue to serve people – and the state has shown that it too strongly resists claims that involve payments. None of this is a sound basis for the report attributing the basest of motives to diocesan officials who were dealing with this matter.

As regards the difficulties professionals face in the protection of children, much more recently, in 2006, Dr Helen Buckley of the Department of Social Studies in Trinity College Dublin wrote in *ChildLinks*, published by Barnardos: '…it has been commented that the 'dysfunction' often attributed to families pales into insignificance when compared with the network of professionals whose responsibility it is to serve them.' If those who are working for the same purpose can be describe as 'dysfunctional', there is little sense in one group, even an official commission of investigation, naming and shaming individuals for failures in which the whole of society has played a part.

5

Chapter 20 of *The Murphy Report*

In March 2013, the trial of Patrick McCabe on charges related to sexual abuse of children concluded in Dublin, following his return from the United States. Chapter 20 of *The Murphy Report,* dealing with his case, was published in full in July 2013. The complete report has now been published.

Media coverage of the report may have helped create an impression that the report is a catalogue of total, unrelieved disaster. Good news is not news – and, of course, no case should be badly handled. In fact, however, the report assessed twenty-seven of the forty-six cases examined as having been handled well, to varying degrees. One case was assessed as inappropriate behaviour and was not included in the sexual abuse cases. The report approved of four of the nineteen earlier cases (Chapters 12-30) and of twenty-three of the remaining twenty-six cases (Chapters 31-57).

(See the summary table of cases in Appendix I.)

The assessments of the commission show significant improvement in the outcomes of the handling of allegations. This is evidence that the diocese learned lessons and that there was a learning curve leading up to the 1996 *Framework Document,* which bore fruit in the handling of cases subsequent to this date.

The report criticised the handling of eighteen cases but in this book I will examine only the case discussed in Chapter 20. Although the commission's assessment is that 'this case encapsulates everything that was wrong with the archdiocesan handling of child sexual abuse cases' (20.176), the evidence documented by the commission itself indicates that the opposite is the case. The reader may be in a position to judge, on the basis of the evidence I present, whether or not the commission's assessment was justified.

Of those priests against whom allegations of abuse were made in the period under investigation, thirty-three were give pseudonyms in *The Murphy Report,* two were left unnamed at the time but have since been named and the remaining eleven were named in the original publication. These priests were the target of anger but the main target of blame in the report and of anger among the public was those in positions of responsibility in the diocese and, to a far lesser extent, those in positions of responsibility in state organisations, the Garda and the Health Service Executive (HSE).

Chapter 20 names nineteen members of Church personnel but no one from among the authorities of the state, except a Garda not directly involved. The report does not explain this puzzling disparity and there are serious questions to be answered about the assessment of the commission in regard to those in positions of responsibility who were named.

It is natural that *The Murphy Report* should have credibility among the public, as it was the result of an enquiry mandated by the government and carried out over several years by a team of highly qualified legal people. But there are important issues at stake, so it is essential, while recognising the emotional impact of the report, to examine its evidence dispassionately and ask whether its conclusions are justified. It is dangerous to presume that any institution or person, Church or state or otherwise, is beyond question or incapable of error.

Chapter 20 is disturbing for a number of reasons:

- The abuse of children reported in this chapter.
- The seemingly total resistance of Patrick McCabe to every effort at control and reform and repentance and the con-

sequent total failure of these efforts.

• How the commission of investigation seems to have lost some necessary objectivity in interpreting the evidence and in offering assessments.

The different sections of the report are available on the Department of Justice website: www.justice.ie. Chapter 20, as well as omitted text from other parts of the report, is available there under the title *Dublin Supplementary Report.*

I will look at how the approach of the Murphy Commission to the question of the 'learning curve' seems to influence the way it views the evidence it presents. We will see too that this view shapes in an extraordinary way the commission's assessment at the end of the chapter.

Before you go any further, you may like to try the following exercise. Read Chapter 20 of *The Murphy Report* for yourself. At sixty-two pages, it is too long to reproduce here but it is available free on line. Start reading on p. 20 and stop just before you come to: 'The commission's assessment'. (20.176)

Then, using your own judgement, make a brief assessment of how the Church and state authorities handled the allegations and dealt with Patrick McCabe, as described in this chapter. The commission's assessment is two hundred and twenty-eight words, including paragraph numbers. Yours could be longer or shorter.

Next, compare your assessment with that of the commission. Finally, when you get a chance, read my chapter and see whether this makes a difference to your own assessment.

An investigation into a rail or air crash does not cast doubt on the fact that the incident occurred: the facts stand. But the investigation can examine, for example, how the authorities dealt with such an event and whether the conclusions and/or assignment of guilt are soundly based on the evidence. Similarly, this commentary on Chapter 20 does not cast any doubt on whether child abuse by clergy of the diocese of Dublin took place. Clearly it did take place. The facts are horrifying and deplorable.

The identification of institutional failures by Church and state in handling allegations of abuse is also vital, both for the vindication of those who were abused and so that society can learn from what went wrong. The Murphy Commission did not have power to impose judicial penalties on institutions or individuals. It did, however, choose to publicly name, blame and shame many individuals in positions of authority in the diocese for failures in dealing effectively with allegations. This is a very real form of penalty. This too can bring a sense of vindication to those who were abused and whose allegations were badly mishandled.

However, the decision by the Murphy Commission to name and blame and shame is problematic, as I hope this commentary will show. It is more problematic again in that Chapter 20 does it in a one-sided way, naming only diocesan officials, not state officials. Those who suffered child sexual abuse wanted to know why it was that the handling of allegations by Church and state authorities was in many cases so disastrous but it would be of no real service to them if aspects of the investigation itself were found to be faulty.

Section: 20.2

In a footnote 66 to 20.2, the commission writes:

> [Father Phelim McCabe] was helpful to his brother but he cannot be held in any way responsible for the manner in which the archdiocese covered up his brother's activities and prevaricated in dealing with him.

This is too simplistic. It is clear from what the commission itself documents in Chapter 20 that the archdiocese tried to deal with the situation in many unsuccessful ways over many years: this is not prevarication.

From whom did the diocese cover up the matter? Reading through Chapter 20, it is difficult to find an instance. From the Gardaí? Although reporting to the Gardaí was one option, there was no legal obligation to do so. One may debate the wisdom of the way the diocese dealt with the situation and it certainly seems that when an abuser was appointed to a new parish the staff there should have been informed of the circumstances. But to interpret it as essentially a sinister covering up of the problem is wholly unsubstantiated. The same applies to the accusation of prevarication.

In 1993, the Department of Justice published a discussion document, *A Proposal for a Structured Psychological Treatment Programme for Sex Offenders*. This document stated: 'There is need for a prison-based structured treatment programme for sex offenders. Such a programme can play an important, though limited, role in helping reduce the extent of sexual victimisation in society.' (p. 31)

In 1994, a sex offender treatment programme was initiated in the Irish prison system for the first time, in Arbour Hill. Patrick McCabe was laicised six years earlier, in March 1988. By then, as well as having been referred for psychiatric help in Dublin, he had been sent for treatment to Stroud in Gloucestershire, New Mexico and London. The diocese was far ahead of the government on the learning curve. The commission should be reporting critically on prevarication by the government and should be loud in praise of the diocese for being so proactive in this matter. It is bizarre that a commission set up by the government should charge the diocese with prevarication.

Government action or inaction was most likely due to the fact that state officials and bodies had very little understanding of what they were facing. If this is a valid excuse for the state, it is equally valid for the Church.

Section 20.16

A former altar boy from the Pro-Cathedral told the commission:

> …for the most part we loved Father McCabe. He just seemed to be a great priest…I was never aware at that time of anything untoward. (20.6)

This was also the impression I formed from my contacts with Pat McCabe. One might interpret this as McCabe's devious way of grooming unsuspecting boys and it is clear from Chapter 20 that McCabe was highly manipulative and resourceful for his own ends. He succeeded in hoodwinking not just diocesan authorities but psychiatrists, psychologists and Gardaí, just as he manipulated the children he abused.

I believe there was a very genuine side to Patrick McCabe's character and that I must find some way to acknowledge that there can be both real goodness and real deviance in a person. I may be criticised for saying that there is goodness in him but it is important for me not to assume that any good traits he showed were simply for deception. I am reminded of St Paul in his *Letter to the Romans* (7:14-25) writing of his own inward struggle: 'Though the will to do good is in me, the power to do it is not… the evil thing which I do not want – that is what I do.' This is true of a priest, just as of any human being. The weight of evil may seem to extinguish goodness yet, though feeling hopeless, we hope. As St Paul writes at the end of *Romans* 8: 'I am certain of this…neither death nor life…not any power, nor any created thing whatever will be able to come between us and the love of God known to us in Christ Jesus.'

That same altar boy from the Pro-Cathedral reported:

...a lot of the kids would never have had a holiday and most people around there wouldn't have had a car...often on Sundays he'd take a combination of the altar boys and some of the local kids from the parish beagling...

When I worked in St Andrew's parish in Westland Row in the 1970s, I used to make a list of names and take small groups of children (with the permission of parents) in my car to the Hell Fire Club in the Dublin mountains in the summer. Fortunately we never had any problem and the children had a lot of fun, as I did myself. When I left Westland Row in 1978, the summer project scheme was making strides, not just there but in many parishes, promoted by the Catholic Youth Council of the diocese (CYC). Many people in Dublin gave of their time on a voluntary basis, including priests, just as all around the country many people devoted energy to sport and activities for children. I never encountered any abuse in any of this.

Child abuse is horrific but one of the unspoken tragedies of the saga of abuse is the collateral damage. Adults who wish only to do their very best for children must now exercise great caution. I hope those children from Westland Row who are now middle-aged have good memories of our visits to the country. It was a different world.

Section 20.17
In relation to the second complaint in 1978, Chapter 20 says:

There is much in the boy's account which was capable of independent verification:

- the fact of his attendance on the particular day in the Pro-Cathedral [for rehearsal for Easter ceremonies]
- his late and lone return to his school

- his presence in Father McCabe's private quarters
- the piece of paper on which Father McCabe noted his details
- the taking of his photograph

There is no evidence that any such enquiries were undertaken.

It is by no means clear why the commission asserts that these elements of the boy's story were capable of 'independent verification':

- The report does not tell us whether the commission checked if the names of the boys who attended in the Pro-Cathedral were noted. Or did they simply assume it?
- His late and lone return to his school would be verifiable only if the school had not yet commenced the Easter break. Does the commission know if this was so?
- His presence in Father McCabe's private quarters was not necessarily verifiable. Presbyteries (the houses of priests) do not normally have a system of monitoring those who enter and leave.
- The piece of paper and the photograph may not have been found for checking. Does the commission know whether or not they were found?

This is not to say that the allegations are untrue but the commission's statement that these items were capable of independent verification is itself in need of verification, which is not offered in the report.

Section 20.18

In relation to the third complaint, in 1978: 'Dr Maurice Reidy, a former staff member of Clonliffe College...had reservations about the woman's capability as a witness.' [Error: Maurice Reidy was Professor of

Moral Theology in Clonliffe, 1973-95.] This does not, of course, mean that he concluded that the allegations were untrue: it was 1977 and Dr Reidy felt the best advice to the woman was 'not to let the priest into her home again'.

In 20.20, the report remarks on 'the woman about whom Dr Reidy was so dismissive'. In hindsight we can see that another course should have been followed but in the context of the time, the report's description of his attitude as 'dismissive' seems unwarranted for an action that would then have seemed proportionate.

Section 20.24

The commission comments on an interview by Canon Ardle McMahon with Patrick McCabe:

> In the circumstances, it was strange that [Father McCabe] was not asked about the context in which he had had a previous need to see a psychiatrist.

Yet in 20.11, Canon McMahon's account is quoted as stating:

> Father McCabe blamed himself for allowing this incident to develop. When he reached home he realised he needed advice and consulted two directors, a spiritual director and a medical one, a psychiatrist I gathered.

Did the commission overlook this?

Sections 20.24 and 20.25

The account of the dealings of Father McCabe with Professor Noel Walsh, Consultant Psychiatrist in St Vincent's Hospital, seems lacking in substance.

The documents do not record what Professor Walsh was told but his subsequent report indicates that he had been told that there had been a number of incidents in which Father McCabe had become attached to young boys and had expressed overt affection for them.

Chapter 20 does not say which 'documents', nor what 'subsequent report', are referred to here: are they diocesan documents? Did Professor Walsh have any documents?

The incidents were attributed to depression. Professor Walsh concluded that Father McCabe should be allowed to continue in pastoral work and to continue to attend him at six-to-eight-weekly intervals on a follow-up basis for six months to a year. The contents of Professor Walsh's report raise the question, once more, as to whether or not Father McCabe was telling the truth about his history of offending, yet there is no evidence that this question was ever asked. Furthermore, there is no evidence to suggest that Father McCabe continued to attend Professor Walsh as recommended.

Chapter 20 does not state whether the commission asked Professor Walsh about these matters, nor about whether the question of doctor-client privilege was relevant. Did the commission draw some unwarranted conclusions on the basis of absence of evidence?

Sections 20.26-20.28

However, a memo written by Archbishop Ryan in 1981 states that, at the time of this [Artane]appointment, he 'spoke to Father McCabe reminding him of the seriousness of his actions and the risk that he ran of imprisonment, quite apart from the scandal that had arisen and the even more public scandal that could arise in the future.'

…This memo indicates that Archbishop Ryan had a fuller understanding of the nature and extent of Father McCabe's problems than other documents might suggest, yet Father McCabe was sent to Artane without any supervision or monitoring of his behaviour. The parish priest was not told of his history. He was allowed to live alone. He was allowed to construct an oratory in the house, where he conducted 'prayer meetings'. He took charge of the altar boys and was given responsibility for parish renewal, all of which gave him ready and unsupervised access to boys.

Could Archbishop Ryan's understanding of the effects of abuse on children have been any better than the contemporary understanding of psychiatrists and psychologists to whom the diocese looked for help? In 1981, how much attention did these professionals pay to the sexually abused child? How much did they know about the abuser?

It appears that, in 1981, Archbishop Ryan was in the vanguard of awareness in Ireland. Why would the commission use this as the basis of a criticism?

Certainly Patrick McCabe's parish priest should have been informed. The commission seems surprised that 'he was allowed to live alone'. Did the commission interpret this as if it were an exception or a special privilege? On the contrary, this was the normal practice in most of the diocese, except, for example, in city-centre parishes like the Pro-Cathedral or Westland Row, where even in a shared house, each priest had his own quarters. In most built-up areas, accommodation for priests in parishes was (and is) a normal semi-detached house. The house is not just a dwelling but a workplace/office. To cater for more than one priest would have required a special build.

The commission seems surprised that 'he was allowed to construct an oratory in the house'. Did the commission check this out, or did they assume that construction was involved? There was no 'construction' involved in the oratory I saw. It was simply a particular use of one room of the house.

Sections 20.30 and 20.31

Father McCabe was in Artane from July 1979 to March 1981 (20.29).

There is evidence that complaints were made to the archdiocese about Father McCabe's behaviour during this period but no investigations such as were previously conducted by Canon McMahon were undertaken, nor was documentary evidence created or maintained in relation to complaints received. The commission has been unable to establish definitively why this was so...

A memo prepared by Archbishop Ryan in March 1981 simply indicates that during Father McCabe's time in Artane other cases were brought to the notice of the archdiocese and that Father McCabe was spoken to and was referred to a psychiatrist and to a psychologist. This psychologist gave evidence to the commission. He was not aware that the referral had come from the archdiocese; he understood the referral had come to him from the psychiatrist. At the time, he did not have expertise in child sexual abuse. The history given to him by Father McCabe is of obsessive thoughts about young boys but no overt sexual behaviour. He described the presenting problem as 'an urge for close physical contact with pre-pubertal boys and while this was not overtly sexual, it was frequently accompanied by ejaculation'. His target group was stated to be nine- to twelve- or thirteen-year-old, good-looking, well-dressed boys. The frequency of incidents was stated to be three to four times per week, with half of the incidents being spontaneous and the other half premeditated. He did not perceive Father McCabe as being a threat to others. He accepts that he was duped by Father McCabe. Father McCabe attended this psychologist between August and October 1980.

Like the psychiatrist, 'Professor (Noel) Walsh concluded that Father McCabe should be allowed to continue in pastoral work' (20.24); here also the psychologist 'did not perceive Father McCabe as being a threat to others.'

Surely it was reasonable for the diocesan authorities to be guided by assurances from those who had more expertise than them in these matters? Would the commission approve if they had rejected these assurances? If professionals in this field could be duped by an abuser, is it difficult to believe that bishops, who were not professionals, could be duped?

Father McCabe also succeeded in getting a favourable report from a psychologist in Sacramento, California, in early 1987. (20.127 and 20.129)

Of particular interest is what the psychologist told the commission: 'At the time, he did not have expertise in child sexual abuse.' The time in question is given: 'Father McCabe attended this psychologist between August and October 1980.' The commission hearings were from 2006 to 2009, more than a quarter of a century later. Did the commission presume that a psychologist at the earlier date would have had such expertise, or did they consider that this psychologist was an exception in not having expertise in child sexual abuse at the time? Did they think to ask whether there was any psychologist in Ireland at the time who had expertise in child sexual abuse? Indeed, any psychologist in the world, given that the field of child sexual abuse was just beginning to be explored in the US, where it had first come to public awareness as a matter for serious study? Did they enquire whether any psychiatrist had any expertise in the field at that time? That a psychologist or psychiatrist would take on such a case is not an indication of expertise in the field as, when such expertise was not even on the radar in the training for psychologists or psychiatrists, not to have the expertise would not have been perceived as a deficiency. To have had the expertise would quite simply be an impossibility. Even more so was this the case for diocesan officials.

Sections 20.35 and 20.36

When it was proposed that Patrick McCabe be sent to a treatment centre in Stroud, one of the preconditions was:

> They required a 'letter of support' from the archdiocese stating that Father McCabe was a priest of the diocese and that the archdiocese would be willing to receive him back as soon as he was judged fit to resume ministry.

There was a presumption among the professionals in Stroud that rehabilitation was possible – this from the reputed 'experts' in the area of paedophilia. Did the commission consider it a failure on the part of diocesan authorities to accept the possibility of rehabilitation?

A second precondition for Stroud was:

> They required a description of his difficulties with some emphasis on 'external damage' done in his ministry. The purpose of this document was to enable them to confront Father McCabe with tangible evidence of the effect of his misconduct on his ministry.
>
> Archbishop Ryan sent a summary of the damage done, with the first point as follows: 'The most distressing feature of Father McCabe's failures is the effect they are likely to have on the young people involved. Apparently their ages range, in so far as I know, is from 6-16.'

Here for the first time, in 1981, we have an indication of Archbishop Ryan's awareness of the damage done to those who were abused. How deep this awareness was is not indicated but it seems that Archbishop Ryan may have been one of the earlier people in Ireland to be concerned about it.

20.37

> The Archdiocese provided Stroud with the name of the psychologist.

Is this an error, when it was the name of Father McCabe's psychiatrist that Stroud required?

20.39

> The Archdiocese told those who enquired about Father McCabe's sudden disappearance that he had gone away for treatment for throat cancer and to ask for prayers for him.

The commission does not provide the evidence for this allegation. Do they have documentary evidence? Did a witness say this? I remember the rumour about cancer at the time but I do not recall anything from the diocese. Has the diocese ever issued statements about the health of clergy, even in reply to enquiries? Was there a statement even at the time Archbishop Kevin McNamara was seriously ill? Could it have been a rumour that Patrick McCabe himself started, as I have heard?

20.40

In an interim report Stroud summarised the position for Archbishop Ryan. The commission gives the date as July 1981 but this may be an error, since the final report (see 20.42 below) is also dated July:

> In conclusion I would say that Father Pat shows a marked improvement over the time he came here. His self-possession and sensitivity has increased and he seems far more mature in his relationships with others. He is much more aware of his weakness and its power over him and wants very much to learn increasing control over it. The extent to which this is still a cerebral understanding and control and to what extent it is a real deep realisation and commitment only

time will show.

At this stage, Stroud was still optimistic, if cautiously so. If diocesan authorities found hope in this that perhaps Father McCabe could change his ways, does the commission consider that at this time the error could have been avoided?

20.41

On the subject of letters to Archbishop Ryan from Father McCabe in Stroud, the report says:

> The over-familiarity in tone and the self-serving pieties are striking. For example, he addressed the Archbishop as 'Dermot', which is very unusual.

It is interesting that the commission regards addressing the Archbishop as 'Dermot' as over-familiar. It would indeed, I think, have been over-familiar were it Archbishop Ryan's predecessor, John Charles McQuaid: it would have invited a swift reprimand. Archbishop McQuaid was commonly referred to as 'John Charles' but I never heard it used to his face! With Archbishop Dermot Ryan, however, there was quite a different relationship. He was ordained a priest in 1950, eleven years before Father McCabe. On the one occasion when I had reason to meet Archbishop Ryan, in 1972, if I recall correctly, I addressed him as 'Dermot', without awkwardness or repercussions. How did the commission come to the conclusion that it was 'very unusual'?

The commission at times seems to regard the relationship between a bishop and priest on the model of employer-employee, or some other secular relationship. This does not at all reflect the reality of a bishop's relationship with a priest who is 'incardinated' into the diocese. The commission would have been well-advised to study Canons 265-272 of Canon Law to have a more realistic appreciation of the relationship. It does not always work at an ideal level, of course, any more than any other human relationship.

On the matter of 'self-serving pieties', examples are given in 20.41: 'In one letter he [Patrick McCabe] compares his experience in Stroud to "Christ's victimhood experience". He also tellingly refers to his stay in Stroud as a "retreat" rather than a course of treatment.' The Murphy Commission would have been well advised to look into commonly accepted expressions of spirituality in that post-Vatican II period: for example, *Christ's Victimhood* is the name of a taped spiritual talk by Archbishop Fulton Sheen, a famous American speaker who died in 1979. Phrases like these may be used in a self-serving way, as can almost any language.

20.42

After Patrick McCabe had had four months of treatment, Stroud issued a final report in July 1981. It stated:

> We feel reasonably confident that he now has the necessary awareness of his particular difficulty and both the knowledge of himself and the resources necessary to make a new and fruitful start on his priestly ministry.
>
> He will undoubtedly need a support system to enable him to continue and deepen the growth that he has begun here and a work environment that does not pose too much of a stress in terms of his particular weakness. While not wanting to appear over-confident with regards to this, we do feel that Father Pat has shown a real desire and determination to take the necessary steps to ensure that it will not continue to pose a real threat to his carrying out of his priestly ministry to which he is clearly deeply committed and called.

With an expression of caution, knowing that there are no guarantees, Stroud is still positive. In the light of this, was it unreasonable of Archbishop Ryan to reappoint Father McCabe in September of that year?

20.45

When appointed to Clogher Road parish in 1981, Father McCabe 'was once again allowed to occupy a house on his own.'

These were simply the normal housing arrangements and it was not a special decision. See 20.26 -28 above.

20.59 and 60

Following a complaint in Clogher Road parish, Father McCabe was sent to the Servants of the Paraclete at Jemez Springs, New Mexico, in July 1982:

> Archbishop Ryan wrote to the director of the programme and enclosed the February 1982 report from Stroud. Unfortunately, the commission did not receive a copy of Archbishop Ryan's letter, so is not aware of what other information was supplied to them.

Chapter 20 does not say whether the commission asked for a copy of the letter in question from Jemez Springs.

> By November 1982, Father McCabe was coming towards the end of his treatment. A decision needed to be taken as to what was to happen next. He wanted to return to Ireland but the psychiatrist in charge of his treatment had reservations because 'he only feels 70 per cent sure that Pat will not get sexually involved with children again. The recidivism rate for people involved with children is very high and also Pat's recidivism history is not good.'

It seems remarkable that the psychiatrist 'only feels 70 per cent sure that Pat will not get sexually involved with children again' — a far lower level of confidence would seem appropriate from a centre with a great deal of experience in the matter.

20.63

At Christmas 1982:

> Father McCabe came back to Ireland for his Christmas holidays. He was not placed under any supervision during his stay. He had access to a car...

As with living alone and having an oratory in his house, it seems strange that the commission would find it unusual that Father McCabe had access to a car. Even if the diocese had forbidden it, the diocese could not enforce this, any more than it could enforce supervision, although indeed some attempt at supervision would have been advisable. Did the commission think in terms of the diocese as a company and a priest as an employee with a company car? The diocese does not supply cars: these are at the personal expense of the priest.

20.64

> The following day, the boy's parents complained to the parish priest, Father Con Curley.

This was 1982. Father Con Curley was curate, not parish priest, in Palmerstown, 1982-93. This error is repeated at 20.92, concerning events in 1986:

> ...the chief superintendent who did not convey them to the investigating garda but who did convey them and the fact of the Garda investigation to his local parish priest, Father Curley.

This chief superintendent is quoted in the same paragraph as saying that it was the local curate, not the parish priest:

...I contacted the local curate who was a very conscientious person
and I knew who would take it on board and he did take it on board...

This may seem trivial, as in the case of Father Reidy at 20.18. But
knowing that a legal document can be rendered void by a single
error of fact, it is extraordinary that the commission shows this
lack of attention to detail and in this case a detail that could have
been checked very simply by referring to diocesan records.

20.67/20.68
Father McCabe returned to Jemez Springs in January 1983, where
he was deemed to be a paedophile and was treated with Depo-
Provera, which 'had been shown in studies in the USA to lessen the
testosterone level and consequently the libido, and therefore was helpful
in controlling the urges of sexual deviants.' (20.68)

(20.100 refers to the insurance policy taken out by the diocese,
which is discussed in Chapter 4 of this book.)

20.155
They (the bishops), in effect, set him loose on the unsuspecting
population of Stockton, California.

This eye-catching but wild hyperbole on the part of the commission implies a malevolent insouciance on the part of the
bishops. It forgets what the commission reported just two
paragraphs earlier, in 20.153:

Monsignor Stenson made enquiries of the Church authorities in
Stockton about the proposed employment. He discovered that
the job involved the housing of homeless people and research
into its causes. The community which was proposing to employ
him consisted of six people, all of whom were adults. There was no

Church link or connection.

20.160

Bishop O'Mahony undertook to send him a copy of his rescript of laicisation. The commission has not seen any evidence that it was in fact sent at this time but Bishop O'Mahony told the commission that he did send it. A copy was sent to Sacramento diocese.

The commission clearly has doubts about this assertion by Bishop O'Mahony. Do we know what reason they had to doubt his word? Do we know whether there was a strict policy in the diocesan administration at the time to record faithfully every piece of correspondence sent? Bishop O'Mahony could not have known at the time that the commission would later expect documentary evidence that the rescript had been sent.

The commission's assessment comes at the end of Chapter 20. In this case, the assessment comprises two hundred and twenty words but it is summarised in the first sentence. I quote the assessment in full:

20.176

This case encapsulates everything that was wrong with the archdiocesan handling of child sexual abuse cases. The story speaks for itself. Archbishop Ryan not only knew about the complaints against Father McCabe, he had a considerable understanding of the effects of abuse on children. This is one of the few cases in which he took a close personal interest. He protected Father McCabe to an extraordinary extent; he ensured, as far as he could, that very few people knew about his activities; it seems that the welfare of children simply did not play any part in his decisions.

20.177

Monsignor Stenson told the commission that 'this case was dreadfully, very poorly handled' and 'a much more decisive decision should have been made earlier.' That, in the commission's view, is a considerable understatement.

20.178

In a saga in which there are very few participants who can be commended, the commission notes the thorough investigation into the first complaint carried out by Canon McMahon and the decisiveness of Bishop Carroll.

20.179

The connivance by the Garda, in effectively stifling one complaint and failing to investigate another and in allowing Father McCabe to leave the country, is shocking. It is noteworthy that the commission would not have been aware of the Garda activity in question were it not for the information contained in the Church files.

In the light of the above commentary on Chapter 20 of *The Murphy Report,* I propose an alternative assessment. These are my words:

Chapter 20 encapsulates very much that was right in the archdiocesan handling of child sexual abuse cases. It also encapsulates much that was wrong with the commission's implementation of its mandate.

The commission does shed much-needed light on the facts of sexual abuse of children and on the handling, especially by Church authorities, but also by state authorities, of allegations and suspicions.

The commission is seemingly oblivious of all the evidence it documents in Chapter 20, which indicates that the diocese expended enormous efforts to deal with Patrick McCabe. The fact that these efforts were in the end entirely ineffective is not to be blamed on diocesan personnel. The real failure would be not to have tried.

Consider a summary of the actions taken by the diocese, as documented in Chapter 20, between the first formal complaint in 1977 and Patrick McCabe's laicisation in 1988, after which it had no control over him.

1977-8
- Interviewed by Canon Ardle McMahon and referred to psychiatrist.

1979-81
- Referred again to a psychiatrist and a psychologist.
- Withdrawn from parish and sent to Stroud, UK, for treatment for four months. Report: 'reasonably confident'.

1982-6
- 'Strenuous efforts' to persuade him to return to Stroud.
- Archbishop removed his faculties to preach, hear confessions and celebrate Mass in public.
- Sent to Jemez Springs, New Mexico, for treatment July-December 1982.
- Return to Jemez Springs 1983: effective house arrest; drug Depo-Provera given in the belief that it helped to control sexual deviance.
- Agreement with Santa Rosa diocese, California, terminates 1986.
- Father McCabe refused appointment in Dublin.

1987
- Father McCabe suspended from ministry.
- Father McCabe applies for laicisation.

March 1988

• The rescript of laicisation comes from Rome:

> As he was laicised, the archdiocese now had no control over him. (20.156)
>
> The Archdiocese spent a total of about £29,000 (€37,000) in treatment and ancillary costs for Father McCabe between the years 1981 and 1987. (20.58)

To describe the above as 'prevarication' or 'cover-up' stretches credibility to breaking point. (20.2, note). What more the diocese (or the state) could have done to try to bring Pat McCabe under control is difficult to know. More could have been done to provide support for the children and the families who made the allegations but, as we know, understanding of the effects on children and of what could be done was still in early stages.

With regard to Monsignor Stenson's judgement of the case, we need to keep in mind firstly that he did not become involved until January 1987 (see 20.119), ten years after the first formal complaint (20.9); and secondly, that when he comes as a witness to the tribunal, about twenty years later, he recalls the facts clearly but is speaking to the commission with hindsight. The members of the commission likewise hear what he says with hindsight.

If Monsignor Stenson's words are interpreted as meaning: that all the efforts ended in failure; that these efforts, undertaken before there were clear procedures and guidelines for dealing with such cases, can now be seen as defective and that with today's knowledge we would make a 'much more decisive' decision earlier; and that the lack of effective action led to Patrick McCabe being enabled to inflict further abuse and suffering, I agree with all these interpretations. But if Monsignor Stenson's words are interpreted as meaning that those in positions of authority in the diocese avoided their responsibilities and consciously chose to cover up the problem with reckless disregard for the consequences, I disagree, on the basis of the evidence presented in Chapter 20 of the report itself.

I cannot say whether or to what extent any person in a position of responsibility in Church or state is culpable: the evidence documented in Chapter 20 is insufficient to warrant any such conclusion. But I can say that any such person who felt that he or she was not treated fairly by the commission was left between the devil and the deep blue sea.

A normal court case is heard in public, the evidence is public and justice may be seen to be done. With a commission of investigation, the hearings are in private. The evidence, except for what the commission may choose to include in its report, remains private, including conflicting evidence. Under Section 42 of the Commissions of Investigation Act 2004, documents of a commission (including its interim, final and draft reports) are absolutely privileged: they have legal immunity from any civil or criminal liability. The possibility of going public with evidence is severely inhibited by the Act, which makes unauthorised disclosure or publication of evidence or documents an offence punishable on conviction on indictment by a fine not exceeding €300,000 or imprisonment for a term not exceeding five years, or both. Witnesses and other individuals have to wait thirty years to go public without penalty.

The commission, having completed its investigation into the diocese of Dublin and issued the report, is now *functus officio*: it has no further function in this matter, so will not respond to my comments. The commission is not a court and it would seem that any possibility of appeal is non-existent.

In Chapter 20 the commission shows a surprising lack of professionalism:

- Those who were abused have been served by bringing some accounts of abuse into the public domain. They have not been well served by serious defects that damage confidence in how well the commission carried out its task. They deserve better.
- The people and priests of the diocese of Dublin have been served by the commission's establishing facts of abuse and how allegations and suspicions were handled by Church and state authorities. They have not been well served by the commission's lack of objectivity in evaluating evidence. Nor have they been well served by the commission's partisan policy of naming only those in positions of responsibility in the diocese, although the people named may have been unable to access the necessary legal protection. They deserve better.
- The people of Ireland whose taxes paid for the commission and for the publication of the report have been served well in that this report, along with the *SAVI* report and other investigations into sexual abuse of children, has made a deplorable dimension of society far more public. This should help to reduce the level of abuse and suffering in coming years. They have not been well served by a report which has not measured up to the professional standards that would be expected. They deserve better.

The commission of investigation was not a court of law but its conclusions against named people are perilously close to a guilty verdict, although the commission had no power to impose penalties as a court might and those named did not have the normal legal defence they would have had in a court of law.

6

Chapter 20: Other Considerations

Naming Individuals

There are many names in Chapter 20. As well as from Father Patrick McCabe, his brother Father Phelim McCabe and another Father Patrick McCabe of the diocese are mentioned in 20.1 and 20.2, in order to avoid confusion. I have counted the names of nineteen other priests (including bishops) of the diocese, while eight other priests are mentioned but not named. Chapter 20 does not give a rationale for keeping these eight names anonymous but it seems to me that those whose names are given had an official function in the diocese in regard to Father McCabe. Those who are not named seem to be friends or other priests who had no official function.

When we come to the Garda, it is more difficult, since in only one case is a name given (20.92), a chief superintendent who owned a house in which Father McCabe was staying and who seems to have had no official function in the matter. In the case of the other Gardaí, those who are not named, it is not always easy to be sure how many people are involved because of their anonymity but as best I can distinguish, there are eleven distinct people, each of whom did have an official function in the investigation of Father McCabe. The DPP's office is also mentioned (20.109 and elsewhere), without any person being named.

An important question, therefore, is why clerics with an official function should be named but no Garda. Unless there is a good explanation, it gives the appearance of selectively targeting clergy. The report does not provide any such explanation.

Sources of Information

The commission received information from witnesses as well as from documentation. The final sentence of Chapter 20 states plainly:

> It is noteworthy that the commission would not have been aware of the Garda activity in question were it not for the information contained in the Church files.

One of the most immediately evident problems with *The Murphy Report* is the disparity in the sources of information for the commission. There is a marked contrast between the way the commission deals with diocesan files and the way it deals with state files. Paragraph 2.18 of the report remarks on the availability of diocesan documentation, including some in digital form.

However, with discovery of documents from the HSE, the work of the commission was not facilitated in the same way. Paragraph 1.98 of the report states:

> The health boards and the HSE do not properly record cases of clerical child sexual abuse.

In the case of the HSE, the commission was told that, because the HSE files were filed by reference to the name of the abused and were not in any way cross-referenced to the alleged abuser, it would have to examine individually up to 180,000 files in order to ascertain whether an alleged abuser was a priest in the Dublin archdiocese (2.19). For this reasons, the commission decided take a 'pragmatic approach' (2.19), relying on the recollections of personnel rather than documents:

Similarly with Garda files: paragraph 2.20 tells us that files were notably deficient from 1975 to 1995, the first twenty years of the period covered, and the commission again resorted to relying on recollections for those years:

> The Garda Síochána gave what documentation they had. This documentation was quite extensive for the period after 1995. They were unable to supply files in relation to some of their activities in the 1960s, 1970s, or 1980s as these had been destroyed or mislaid. Members of the force who had been involved in cases about which the commission had queries and for which the files were missing or destroyed gave evidence of their recollections of those cases.

A significant imbalance results from the 'pragmatic approach' of the commission in relation to the HSE and the Garda files. Handling of allegations by Church authorities received far more attention. Even if all the commission's unfavourable judgements of the diocese were soundly based, the very fact that the Church documents provided so much information puts diocesan officials very much at a disadvantage

This leads to a further difficulty, that the diocese was judged without a comparable 'control group' to indicate how handling of abuse allegations by the diocese compared with their handling by state authorities in the context of the knowledge and under-standing of the times. It seems extraordinary that the files of statutory bodies of government should be less well kept than those of a diocese. All organisations dealing with children need to have their handling investigated. We cannot know whether the way the diocese handled allegations was better or worse than in society in general, unless other organisations are also investigated. It is as important to do this as it is to evaluate the handling in the context of the knowledge and understanding that prevailed at the period in question.

Manipulation and Other Agendas

It seems that Patrick McCabe was highly manipulative, a characteristic that appears to occur frequently in those who abuse children.

We must remember, however, that most of us at one time or another use manipulation in order to convey the information or impression we want, while omitting information that does not serve our purpose. This does not necessarily mean we set out to deceive: it is more that we try to judge what will bring about the result we want. The Church authorities chose to handle matters in a particular way. They have frequently been accused of 'cover-up'. I am sure that they had in mind the scandal to the good name of the Church and the possible repercussions. Commercial bodies, political parties and other organisations or individuals do likewise. But I am also sure that diocesan officials had very much in mind what they could do to bring Patrick McCabe back to a non-abusive way of life.

If the diocese had at the very first complaint expelled McCabe from the priesthood and passed matters over to the state authorities, what would those authorities have done? Would they have handled the matter more effectively? Where would Patrick McCabe be now? A limited prison sentence would have taken him out of circulation for a while but it seems likely that this would not have prevented him going on to inflict further suffering by abusing others. Who can say whether the result would have been better or worse than sending him for whatever help and treatment was available at the time and keeping some semblance of control through his desire to continue in the priesthood?

Unless there are other provisions of civil law under which the abuse falls, it seems clear that the diocesan authorities did not put themselves above civil law in not reporting the cases to the Garda. The report states that at that time, 'There was no legal requirement for such reporting.' (1.16) There were people who came first to the diocese specifically because they did not want to approach the Garda.

One may say that the diocesan authorities covered up and did not act as they should but I believe this is too simplistic an assessment. I believe they did all in their best judgement at the time to try to bring Father McCabe to repentance and to resume active ministry as a priest.

One must also ask about the agendas of other players in the sorry saga: the Garda, the HSE, the media, the government, the various support and lobby groups and the commission of investigation itself. This is not to say that they were dishonest but they too acted out of their own specific interests. When there were no clear legal or pastoral guidelines or procedures for dealing with abuse of children, it was understandable that the diocese would try to fix it locally.

One must ask the question: how did the Murphy Commission carry out its function? Did it act always within natural and constitutional justice and within the terms of the Act under which it was set up? The members of the commission were legal people. How was this a factor in the way they approached their work? Was the Commissions of Investigation Act 2004, under which it was established, a suitable foundation?

The Murphy Report (1.7) makes clear that the commission was aware of the limits of its mandate:

> This Commission's investigation is concerned only with the institutional response to complaints, suspicions and knowledge of child sexual abuse.

Given this mandate, were they justified in naming and shaming people and in doing so selectively?

Among the various apparent errors of fact and judgement on the part of the commission which I have noticed, I have found no instance where the error appeared to favour a diocesan official.

It may be argued that many of the criticisms I have listed here are insubstantial. Some, indeed, are slight. But the fact that there are errors, slight or major, in a document of such importance seems to indicate a lack of due care on the part of the commission. It may be that the commission members were under pressure to work through a vast number of documents and other evidence. It must have been harrowing to work for over three years on data documenting so much abuse and failure. Perhaps the commission lacked sufficient time to eliminate the errors. Or perhaps the sense of horror among members of the commission at the catalogue of abuse unwittingly coloured their judgement of the handling of allegations.

There are so many errors in just one chapter of *The Murphy Report* that cumulatively they cannot be ignored.

The Focus of Concern

With regard to Patrick McCabe, one might be tempted to say that when all attempts at reform and restoration fail, the only alternative is retribution: put the abuser in prison and throw away the key. But this 'solution' is not open to any of the authorities involved. For the Church, the mission is that of Jesus: rebirth, a call to a new way of life, even or especially for those who seem beyond help or redemption.

The commission: 'has been impressed by the extraordinary charity shown by complainants and their families towards offenders…Many indeed expressed concern for the welfare of the priest concerned.' (1.105)

This concern was shared by diocesan officials. It was shown by the attention paid to bringing about a change of behaviour, repentance and forgiveness. Removal from office was a last resort.

The Murphy Commission charged that: 'The welfare of children, which should have been the first priority, was not even a factor to be considered in the early stages.' (1.113)

It is all very well for us today, with our improved understanding, to say that the welfare of children should have been the priority but, in the 1970s and 1980s, a child presenting with allegations of sexual abuse or an adult reporting having been abused as a child would have had difficulty finding informed help. The deeper and more long-term effects of sexual abuse were yet to be established.

How the abuse can affect the family of an abused child is also a complex issue. They can struggle with a sense of helplessness and a sense of failure to protect their child even though they themselves are entirely blameless. When they turn to trusted authorities for help and find no support, the situation becomes even more hopeless. Sometimes a child may report the abuse to a parent and be met with disbelief, or even with punishment.

The dilemma for family and friends of the abuser is how they can still be family for the abuser, who may resist all attempts at any treatment or help and who may spend some years in prison.

This in some way parallels the dilemma for the Church community. Where a priest sexually abuses a child, is there anything those in authority can do to reform and restore the abuser? Does there come a stage in an individual case where those with responsibility for the situation in the Church must accept that there is simply no more that they can do and expel the abuser from the priesthood? Is there some way the Church can instead be a safeguarding community for the abuser? Chapter 20 of *The Murphy Report* (and, indeed, the whole report) shows little understanding of the specific mission of the Church.

Selective Targeting

It is a matter of grave concern that, although the commission was mandated to investigate how both Church and state handled allegations, Chapter 20 names only the diocesan personnel.

In 20.179, they are critical of the Garda:

The connivance by the Garda in effectively stifling one complaint
and failing to investigate another and in allowing Father McCabe to
leave the country is shocking.

Yet no Garda, except one who was not involved in the investigation, is named in Chapter 20. How could the commission have
been so selective as to choose to identify 'culprits' on only one
side?

The Murphy Commission has the benefit of hindsight. In
Chapter 20 it errs seriously in exercising that hindsight only to
judge negatively. In its summary, there is no acknowledgment of
all the efforts the diocese made to try to remedy the dreadful
wrong, even if they were totally unsuccessful. If it were the state
authorities, would they have expended such time and resources?
Would they even have considered sending Patrick McCabe to
Stroud and to New Mexico, to centres that were specialist in
dealing with this type of offender? The state did not introduce its
first treatment programme for sex offenders in prison until 1994.
Indeed, it would be interesting to know what other organisations
would have done if the first formal complaint in Patrick McCabe's
case had come to them in 1977 or in the years following.

With the assurances received from professionals in the fields
of psychology, psychiatry and abuse, are diocesan authorities to
be condemned for acting on the best advice they could find at the
time? There would be better grounds for criticism if they had not
sought the professional advice, or if they had overruled it.

All the efforts to rehabilitate Father McCabe detailed in
Chapter 20, although unsuccessful, are clear evidence that the
diocese took the matter very seriously. One can well understand
the frustration of Archbishop Ryan (20.53):

'In the name of God, what does one do with a man like that? And to suggest sending him away, he's quite liable to say no. And what does one do then?'

If the commission examined only the institutional failures, there would be less cause for concern, but it chose to name diocesan officials in Chapter 20. According to Sections 11 and 12 of the 2004 Act, witnesses at the commission were entitled to know only the substance of evidence given by another witness concerning them, not the full account. Whether they would be told the source of this evidence was at the discretion of the commission. In such a situation, it would be very difficult to rebut any evidence. In addition, a witness could be cross-examined by or on behalf of a person only if the commission so directed (Section 11, 2(c)).

If it were the intention of the commission to name individuals, resulting perhaps in serious damage to their reputation, they should surely be afforded all necessary means of defence. The question must be asked whether the Commissions of Investigation Act 2004 is an appropriate legal foundation for the kind of investigation that was carried out by the Murphy Commission. That is a question for those with legal expertise.

Means of Defence

If some diocesan personnel felt they had not been treated fairly, why did they not take court action to rectify it? Section 35 of the 2004 Act, summarised, makes the following provision:

A person receiving such a draft who believes that fair procedures have not been observed can either:

• Make a written submission to this effect to the commission and hope that they will make the required amendments

or

- Apply to the court for an order directing the commission to amend its report

Once they have received a submission, the commission may take one of three steps: amend the report; apply to the court for directions; or decide not to make any amendments.

One is faced with a choice: one may take a chance that the commission will respond effectively, knowing that one has no avenue of appeal if it makes no amendment. Alternatively, one can apply to the court. This may seem the obvious choice. However, an important consideration is the prohibitive cost, both financial and personal, of taking court proceedings. There will also be the possibility, even the likelihood, of bitterly negative media coverage, despite the fact that recourse to the court is a legal right and that one's reputation is at stake. One need only recall the media reaction when Cardinal Connell exercised his legal right to protect some documents. It was immediately interpreted almost universally as a further attempt at cover-up to protect himself and the diocese, although legal privilege in a document is there not to protect the person with the document but the client whose confidential information is contained in it.

As an agency of the state, the commission was bound by the provision of Article 40.3.2 of the Constitution: 'The State shall, in particular, by its laws protect as best it may from unjust attack and, in the case of injustice done, vindicate the life, person, good name and property rights of every citizen.' In this case, however, it appears that the commission was able to attack the good name of citizens with impunity, while it was made very difficult for them to defend their good name. Diocesan authorities tried to deal with this difficult case and failed. Would the state have done any better, faced with the same situation? Was there a better way at the time?

The commission comments:

> In a saga in which there are very few participants who can be commended, the commission notes the thorough investigation into the first complaint carried out by Canon McMahon and the decisiveness of Bishop Carroll. (20.178)

Why is it that, apart from this one remark, the commission is almost unremittingly negative about measures taken by the diocese?

Why is it that, although it provides so much evidence of efforts by the diocese to deal with the abuser, it all seems to count for nothing except as evidence of prevarication and self-serving?

The Murphy Commission operates in a delicate area of relations between Church and state. A comment of the commission at 1.55 seems to come perilously close to going beyond its limits for a government-appointed commission:

> As an organisation operating within society, it seems to the commission that the Church ought to have some regard to secular requirements in its choice of leader.

As it happens, I agree with the opinion expressed here. The appointment of bishops is an area that needs to be reformed. Were an individual or a Church organisation to express this opinion, it would seem perfectly normal. But for a government-appointed commission make such a comment raises problems. Imagine how strongly both the state and the media would react if the Catholic hierarchy or a body appointed by them were to express the opinion: 'It seems to us that the state ought to have some regard to religious requirements in its choice of leader.'

There is enough evidence in just this one chapter to indicate that there is ground for criticism of the report. I cast no doubt whatsoever on the truth and reality of the sexual abuse which gave rise to *The Murphy Report*. I cast no doubt on the suffering which resulted from the continued failure to find effective means to deal with the allegations. I do not attempt to imply that everything was good about the handling of allegations by the diocese. I do not question the need for such a report, which, I believe, has made a valuable contribution to our understanding of child sexual abuse.

It is clear, too, that a compassionate listening and effective response was tragically absent in many cases. The question is whether this was due to the listeners disregarding those who were abused and their overriding desire for self-protection, or whether it can be attributed to a lack of understanding of the serious consequences of the abuse and a lack of awareness of the necessary procedures to deal with the situation.

A question arises also about the quality of the psychiatric and therapeutic advice the diocese received, an area which receives little attention in the report, as well as the legal advice the diocese may have received, and whether those responsible for this advice also bear responsibility for the failures. These are areas that the report fails to address.

It is remarkable that a report produced by a professional legal team should contain so many defects. All these considerations suggest that we must consider seriously whether the report, as represented in Chapter 20, is the report we should have received, the report we still need.

'Cover-up'

One of the most damning paragraphs in *The Murphy Report* overall is in the conclusion to Chapter 1, at paragraph 1.113 (my emphasis):

> The commission has no doubt that clerical child sexual abuse was *covered up* by the archdiocese of Dublin and other Church authorities over much of the period covered by the commission's remit. The structures and rules of the Catholic Church facilitated that *cover-up*. The State authorities facilitated the *cover-up* by not fulfilling their responsibilities to ensure that the law was applied equally to all and allowing the Church institutions to be beyond the reach of the normal law enforcement processes. The welfare of children, which should have been the first priority, was not even a factor to be considered in the early stages. Instead the focus was on the avoidance of scandal and the preservation of the good name, status and assets of the institution and of what the institution regarded as its most important members – the priests. In the mid 1990s, a light began to be shone on the scandal and the *cover-up*. Gradually, the story has unfolded. It is the responsibility of the state to ensure that no similar institutional immunity is ever allowed to occur again. This can be ensured only if all institutions are open to scrutiny and not accorded an exempted status by any organs of the state.

In the above paragraph the term 'cover-up' occurs four times. Apart from condemning the horror of the abuse itself, the phrase 'cover-up' was perhaps the one most commonly used by media and public to condemn the handling by the diocese of the allegations, almost as a kind of shorthand for all that was wrong in the diocese in this matter. The phrase carries implications not just of secrecy but of culpable and reckless disregard in pastoral care, arising from concern with

> ...the avoidance of scandal and the preservation of the good name, status and assets of the institution and of what the institution regarded as its most important members – the priests.

and as a consequence:

> The welfare of children, which should have been the first priority, was not even a factor to be considered in the early stages.

For this reason, we need to examine closely the significance of the expression 'cover-up'.

The phrase also occurs in paragraphs 1.35, 1.102 and 16.53 of the report, while in Chapter 20, in relation to the case of Father Patrick McCabe, a footnote to paragraph 2 mentions 'the manner in which the archdiocese covered up his brother's activities and prevaricated in dealing with him' in relation to Patrick McCabe's brother Phelim. While exonerating Father Phelim McCabe, the commission issues a general condemnation of the archdiocese for the way it 'covered up' and 'prevaricated'. Yet, on reading Chapter 20, it is difficult to find any account of covering up, except in a failure to notify a parish priest of Father McCabe's history. Perhaps the commission interprets as a cover-up the efforts of the diocese to deal with the situation without handing the whole thing over to state authorities, but at the time there was no legal obligation to do this.

The diocese's exhaustive efforts to deal with the situation, as documented in Chapter 20, are clear evidence that there was no prevarication.

We know from material to which I referred earlier (McKeown and Gilligan's report) that referrals for child sexual abuse known to health authorities between 1984 and 1987 totalled 1726. I have been unable to find Garda statistics for child sexual abuse for those years. If the health authorities failed to report those 1726 cases to the Gardaí, would the Murphy Commission charge them with cover-up?

The earliest sexual abuse statistics I have found for the Garda are from the Central Statistics Office for 2003*:

	Recorded	Detected
Total Sexual offences	1968	1248
0212 Defilement of a boy or girl less than 17 years old	132	90
0221 Incest	4	4

The total of recorded cases of 'defilement', plus incest, for 2003 is 136. This is just 8.26 per cent of the number recorded by the health authorities sixteen years earlier, in 1987. Why so much lower? One would have expected the number to have increased significantly by 2003 rather than dropped by 91.74 per cent. It seems clear that reporting to Gardaí, at least in the past, was not common, even for a state agency.

The *SAVI* report (2002) comments (p. 9): 'While recorded crime numbers have increased, there remains the concern that there is significant under-reporting of abuse and in particular a shortfall in seeking legal redress. Dublin Rape Crisis Centre figures from 1998–2000 showed that only a quarter of counselling clients for child sexual abuse had reported the abuse to the Gardaí (19 per cent in 1998-9 and 23 per cent in 1999-2000), while a third of those seeking counselling for adult sexual assault had reported to

---

* www.cso.ie

the Gardaí (36 per cent in 1998/9 and 33 per cent in 1999/2000) (DRCC, 2000; DRCC, 2001).'

Statistics from Garda records for 2011 (from the Central Statistics Office) show that the number of recorded offences of 'defilement' of a boy or girl younger than seventeen years old, and incest, was 153. Statistics from the Dublin Rape Crisis Centre for the same year show that the centre had 9085 genuine counselling contacts, of which 47% related to child sexual abuse. This works out at a total of 4264, twenty-eight times the Garda number, if we understand 'defilement' as having roughly the same meaning as sexual abuse. Even though it is likely that some children contacted DRCC more than once, the difference is still remarkable. This indicates that a very large number of those who contacted DRCC never contacted the Gardaí. Is this a cover-up?

Given that callers to DRCC may remain anonymous, a very large proportion of those who contact the centre may wish to avoid coming to Garda notice, so approach the centre for support in the trust the case will not be reported to the Gardaí. Only a quarter of child sexual abuse clients in the DRCC, 1998–2000, had reported the abuse to the Gardaí. In the case of the other three-quarters, we do not know whether the RCC reported the abuse. If they did not, would the Murphy Commission charge them with cover-up?

If there was so little reporting to the Gardaí, we might ask: who was reporting child sexual abuse to them? Was anybody reporting? With so few cases, could it be that virtually all the Garda cases were ones that were not reported to them by another person but cases of which they themselves became aware in their regular work?

This prompts the question: if so few were reporting to the Gardaí, does it mean that the vast majority of Irish people did not consider that the Gardaí were the appropriate people to whom abuse should be reported? Did the Gardaí themselves at the time consider that they were the appropriate people to whom such abuse should be reported? We have an indication of how this was understood at 20.92 of *The Murphy Report*, when Garda Chief Superintendent Joe McGovern told the commission:

> I didn't report – I didn't consider it appropriate to notify the local gardaí in case – they could even think I was meddling. I took the course that I thought was the proper course at the time. I contacted the local curate who was a very conscientious person and I knew who would take it on board and he did take it on board and he got onto the Archbishop's House about the matter and he subsequently told me that he got onto the superintendent in Ballyfermot. So I think there was no omission on my part there.

Garda work is not carried out in isolation but in cooperation with the society and communities the force serves. If the commission wishes to interpret this comment as undue deference to the Church, it will need to establish the following:

- That at the time Gardaí adopted this policy only in regard to the Catholic Church, not in regard to other religious bodies, nor in regard to non-religious bodies, statutory or voluntary
- That there was a better way of dealing with the issue at the time, that it was known and understood in the Garda at the time and that there was appropriate training either of Gardaí in general or of a specialised group within the force

The report establishes neither of these conditions. There is no record in the report of the commission enquiring what kind of competence or training in this matter was available to Gardaí at the time. What guidelines and procedures, if any, did Gardaí have for dealing with child sexual abuse in the 1960s, 1970s, 1980s and 1990s? Without knowing these essential facts, the commission does not have a solid foundation for criticising Garda action or inaction. Nor does it have a solid foundation for concluding that the way Dublin diocese handled allegations was worse than their handling would have been by Gardaí or state authorities, or by other organisations.

Perhaps what has been called 'undue deference to the Church' was merely on a par with how the Gardaí might turn to the Rape Crisis Centre to deal with the situation, or to the Department of Health itself, or to some other body? If the Gardaí received a report of abuse concerning a child of the Church of Ireland or the Presbyterian or Methodist Church, or of the Jewish community, or of some other faith body, how did they act? Did officials of these churches or congregations report such matters to the Gardaí? While relative numbers may be smaller, we cannot presume that abuse did not occur in these communities, according to the information provided by the *SAVI* report.

There may be a perception that sexual abuse of children exists principally in the Catholic Church and especially among priests. While there is no doubt that the problem exists in the Catholic Church, it is not consistent with the facts to see it mainly in these terms. It is a problem in society. Otherwise why would so many other organisations have produced guidelines for safeguarding children in recent years? Why would the Irish government have published *Children First: National Guidance for the Protection and Welfare of Children* (latest edition 2011), in which the only reference to the Catholic Church is on p. 67 where, among many other references, it lists the publication *Safeguarding Children: Standards and Guidance Document for the Catholic Church in Ireland* (Maynooth, 2009)?

Is it possible that what the report calls 'institutional immunity' and 'exempted status' (1.113) in relation to the Church were simply the accepted way for members of the Garda to act at the time? Was it simply the practice that when a case came before a local station, it was up to the local sergeant or to the Garda on duty to decide, in the absence of recognised procedures, how best the abused child could be helped?

We might also ask how the Gardaí as a body handled cases where the abuser was a member of the Gardaí. What if the child of a Garda were abused? How would a Garda deal with the situation if the child who was abused were a child of a Garda and the abuser was within the family? It may be impossible to find answers to these questions but we cannot presume, just because Catholicism was the majority religion of the state, that the Church was treated differently – nor can the commission to so presume.

In May 2012, an Irishman with a high public profile spoke on Newstalk about his experience of being abused as a child. (Yes, I know his identity and I'm covering it up.): 'I was sexually abused in 1961 and I was physically abused in 1963. I was eleven and thirteen respectively at the time. I knew what it was, I knew it was abuse. When I told my father about it he knew it was abuse and he knew exactly what action had to be taken.'

He did not specify what he meant by saying that his father 'knew exactly what action had to be taken'. Perhaps his father reported the abuse to the Garda. But I know that, then and now, the first 'action' to come to many people's minds would not be to report it to the Garda. Many Irish people – and indeed this may also be true of other jurisdictions – have an ambiguous relationship with the Gardaí. This it not in any way a criticism of the Gardaí, just an observation. A Garda is an authority figure who has power to do things, things I may not like. Perhaps it is different for people in the legal profession who may be perfectly at home dealing with Gardaí. For most people, when a Garda is dealing with someone else, that's fine. But dealing with you – not quite so relaxed? If, while driving, you see a parked Garda car or a checkpoint a short distance ahead, do you instinctively take your foot off the accelerator and check what speed you're doing? Do you ask yourself when you last checked your headlights and tail lights? What about your tyres?

As for going to the Gardaí about a sexual matter: how many Garda stations have a comfortable room where you can have a private conversation about very embarrassing and sensitive personal matters? Especially for a child, being brought to a Garda station could well be very threatening, since the child might feel that he or she was being brought there for doing something wrong. As for asking a Garda to come to the house in this kind of matter, that's even worse: even if they come in plain clothes, they may be recognised. And will they ask you whether you can give them the names of any witnesses? Will they be looking to find out whether you have anything to hide – any way you may have been even partially responsible? A person who is sexually abused may feel ashamed and guilty, even though they are not in any way responsible. In this situation, we cannot expect the person or his or her family to act in the most rational way. There is great difficulty, too, if the abuser is a member of the family. It can be much easier to go to a doctor or a priest. If the doctor or priest advises the person to report it to the Gardaí? Absolute refusal would not be unusual – or reluctant agreement, with failure to follow through. How does 'cover-up' fit into these situations?

It is all very well for a person in high position to say, 'You must do this!' On the ground, the situation is far more confused. Human beings in stressful situations are far more complex. I do not argue whether or not it is best to report all cases of allegations of child sexual abuse to the Gardaí. The best policy is in this matter has been disputed and seems to have been resolved now in the direction of always reporting. What I do argue is that church authorities should not be judged in this matter by criteria to which other bodies are not held. The Murphy Commission presumes far too easily that motives in Dublin diocese are suspect and charges the diocese with cover-up. This is a logical consequence of how *The Murphy Report* starts, with attacking the motives and credibility and trustworthiness and truthfulness of diocesan officials at 1.14, when the commission, without foundation, rejects the assertion by diocesan officials that they were on a learning curve.

Procedures in the Church work with various levels of confidentiality. One may question whether this confidentiality is wise. If confidentiality in church administration is interpreted as a detestable cover-up, how are we to interpret the ban in the 2004 Act on disclosure of any of the evidence of the commission of investigation? On the basis of the many defects in *The Murphy Report,* one might argue that the thirty-year embargo on release of commission documents should be lifted immediately, to allow proper debate.

Is it ever legitimate to conceal the truth? *The Murphy Report* itself conceals facts, most obviously in the assigning of pseudonyms to priests in thirty-five of the forty-six cases examined. Father McCabe, the subject of Chapter 20, was not even given a pseudonym in the original publication: the space was simply left blank. The report says, in a footnote to 1.12: '*Names marked with an asterisk are pseudonyms.' It gives no reason. One may presume that the commission used this device in order to avoid legal difficulties were a case to come to court.

Why then did the commission presume that when officials in the diocese kept matters confidential, it was for nefarious rather than good reasons? It must have been obvious to the commission that the pastoral work of the diocese could not continue unless the people whom the diocese serves had real trust in priests of the diocese being committed to confidentiality in what they hear. Much of this work involves personal information that the person would not want to be publicised; it can also include information about wrongdoing. People who approached the diocese alleging cases of abuse sometimes chose to do this rather than go to the Garda. If the diocese is to be condemned for not passing the allegation on to the Garda, why should the people who brought the allegation to the diocesan authorities not also be condemned for not going to the Garda directly?

Medical and legal professionals and social workers may also be aware of evidence of wrongdoing – which at times may include child sexual abuse – but they have their own codes of confidentiality for good reason. Yet the commission seems to interpret such aspects of the work of the diocese in relation to child sexual abuse, even before the 1996 *Framework Document*, as reprehensible.

'Cover-up' is used to describe an attempt, whether successful or not, to conceal evidence of wrong-doing, error, incompetence or other embarrassing information when the person (or commission in this case) believes that it is done without good reason. It can be done either by denying the matter in hand, or by acknowledging it while simultaneously distracting attention from the matter in such a way that it goes unnoticed, such as when a newspaper is obliged to publish a retraction or apology for an item that had been mis-reported but manages to present it in such a way that in attracts very little attention: for example, by 'burying' it at the bottom of an inside page or distracting from it by running a major story with a big headline on the same page. If a government knows that its military actions have caused the deaths of non-combatants and it denies that these actions took place, this is a cover-up. If a tobacco company knows that smoking damages health but refuses to acknowledge it, this is a cover-up. If a pharmaceutical company knows that a particular medication has serious side-effects but denies it, this is a cover-up.

The question in this instance is whether diocesan officials, without good reason, deliberately concealed important matters in the various cases of child sexual abuse. I cannot say that there was no element whatsoever of what the commission refers to as 'cover-up'. The question is whether any such practice of confidentiality was carried out in a manner that endangered children, when diocesan officials knew they should have acted in a different manner, or whether the maintenance of confidentiality was justified in the circumstances of each case. Tragically, we know, children did suffer. Did diocesan officials know that they should have taken a different course of action? Did they show reckless disregard for the safety of children? It seems clear that the Murphy Commission has used the 'cover-up' charge in a far broader manner than that justified by the evidence presented by the commission itself.

If a charge of cover-up is to be substantiated, I would suggest that these three elements are required:

- That the person concerned knows the facts sufficiently clearly
   and
- That the person concerned knows sufficiently clearly what to do about it, whether to act to remedy it, or whether to report to appropriate authorities
   and
- That the person concerned decides, despite the above, deliberately not to take the required action and/or to take alternative action which does not remedy the injustice but allows or facilitates its continuance.

Firstly, in the matter of knowing the facts of child sexual abuse, there are significant difficulties. To establish the facts in such cases is notoriously difficult, because of the secrecy involved and the relationships which may be affected. Families can be destroyed. Sigmund Freud (1856-1939), in the early days of psychoanalysis, encountered accounts of child sexual abuse from adult clients and reported his findings, which were not well received, for whatever reason; he later changed to wondering whether the accounts were delusional. We have him to thank for drawing attention to the possible effects of abuse for the abused person in later life. But even he has been accused by some of covering up child abuse. After his time, there seems to have been little attention paid to the long-term effects, until the setting up of the first rape crisis centres in USA in the early 1970s, which saw people coming for help for the abuse suffered in their childhood. This reignited the present phase of attention to and study of the whole matter.

In dealing with child sexual abuse, while recognising the awful reality of the abuse, we must be aware of the damaging effects of untrue allegations. For an innocent person to have an allegation of child sexual abuse made against them is in itself a horrifying experience. If the relevant authorities immediately remove that person from their position, it adds to the trauma. There is further severe stress in the protracted waiting for the state and the Church authorities to conclude their procedures on the allegation. Finally, if and when the person is declared by both authorities to be innocent of all charges, it may be impossible to restore the person's reputation before the public. The reporting of the finding of innocence will rarely be given the kind of prominence that the original allegation was given. If the original false allegation was made by a media organisation which then decides to fight its corner tooth and nail, even a declaration of innocence in court could never compensate for the trauma.

Secondly, the next step, knowing what to do about it, may be fairly clear to us today (although not undisputed) but, before the publication of the Church's *Framework Document* in 1996 there were no clear agreed guidelines. Actions of the diocese before this date should not be assessed in the same way as its actions after publication of the document. 'Cover-up' is certainly not an appropriate way to describe actions taken in the context of their time which genuinely sought to find the best way of dealing with the matter.

The serious lack of historical perspective on the part of the commission has had devastating consequences. In *The Irish Times* of Tuesday 30 July 2013, Fintan O'Toole wrote in an Opinion piece entitled 'Ten Socially Destructive Acts to Commit with Impunity': '8: Covering up and repeatedly facilitating sexual attacks on children by known predatory paedophiles. (Several Irish bishops, *The Murphy Report*.)'

In the same issue of the newspaper, he is reported as having told the MacGill summer school: 'No bishop has been prosecuted for facilitating child rape.'

This prominent journalist's understanding of *The Murphy Report* and various media investigations appears to be that bishops have been responsible for covering up and facilitating sexual attacks on children and for facilitating child rape. To what extent does he reflect a common public perception? What factors have contributed to this public perception? Has *The Murphy Report* played a major role in creating this perception?

In her book, *Child Sexual Abuse and the Catholic Church,* Marie Keenan makes some remarks on this matter of 'cover-up':

'The conventional explanation of the hierarchy's response to the problem of sexual abuse in the Catholic Church has become a theory of 'cover-up' – a theory the simplicity of which is intuitively compelling and socially supported. However, this theory also requires further scholarly analysis. The gap in the data on this topic is important, as the data on which to base good analysis are hard to come by. In other organisations where there are allegations of wrongdoing, the power, boundaries and secrecy of the organisation have either restricted or completely prevented researchers from gaining access to information about leadership and decision-making.' (p. 181)

'...it was only in 1995 that officials in the archdiocese of

Dublin first began to notify the civil authorities and the police of complaints of child sexual abuse against its priests. The (Murphy) report did not contextualise this finding in relation to reporting practices in other organisations and institutions in Ireland for child sexual offences during the relevant period.' (p. 191)

There is far more investigation required into this question of cover-up to reach a more balanced assessment than the one we find in *The Murphy Report* and in the remarks of Fintan O'Toole. The question of child sexual abuse has had such publicity in the past twenty years that it can be difficult for people today to realise how little it impinged on public consciousness before then.

Another question which is relevant to the area of confidentiality is in relation to data protection legislation. Section 39 of the Commissions of Investigation Act 2004 states: 'Section 4 of the Data Protection Act 1988 does not apply to personal data provided to a commission' under specified conditions. Legal expertise is required here. To what extent was the information in the 70,000 diocesan files which were given to the commission subject to data protection legislation? If a person approached the diocese about child sexual abuse and the diocese kept a file on this, was the diocese acting in accordance with the law when it handed over the file? Whatever 'legal privilege' (if that is the correct term) attaches to the information, it is not primarily for the protection of the person or organisation holding the information but for the protection of the 'client'. Should the clients concerned have been asked for permission? Was their permission required to hand over the file? Would the diocese have been within its rights in refusing to hand over certain files? Would the person who made the allegation, rather than the diocese as the data holder, be within his/her rights in refusing permission? In September 2013, Claire Loftus, the Director of Public Prosecutions, wrote in the Foreword to the 2012 *Annual Report* of her office (my emphasis):

'As reported elsewhere in this report the Office continues

to work with various agencies in the criminal justice system to improve the delivery of services to victims of crime. I was very pleased that in 2012 the Office entered into a Protocol with the Dublin Rape Crisis Centre for access to relevant documents that they hold which are required for the purposes of disclosure in criminal proceedings. *Such protocols, which of course operate on the basis of the consent of the victim,* help to clarify the respective positions of the Office and the agency assisting victims and have in my view streamlined the whole disclosure process.'*

Did the Murphy Commission seek any such consent from those who approached the diocese with complaints of sexual abuse?

If the first two of these elements are verified: that the person concerned knows the facts sufficiently clearly; and knows sufficiently clearly what to do about it either to act to remedy it or to report to appropriate authorities; and if the person concerned then decides, despite the above, deliberately not to take the required action and/or take alternative action which does not remedy the injustice but allows or facilitates its continuance despite being in a position to take remedial action, then we have a clear case of 'cover-up', regardless of what the motives may be.

In the case of Chapter 20 of *The Murphy Report* and, I suggest, in most of the cases covered by the report, the first two conditions are not verified.

The statement of the commission, that 'in the mid 1990s, a light began to be shone on the scandal and the cover-up' (1.113), is not true to the historical facts. Rather, in the mid 1990s, much improved knowledge and understanding of the nature of child sexual abuse, of the effects of the abuse on the child and of more effective ways of dealing with the abusers began to shine a light on the prevalence of child sexual abuse and on the failures in the past to deal with it. Child sexual abuse is a great tragedy and injustice.

---

* www.dppireland.ie

It is a scandal if there was deliberate negligence in applying the best current knowledge and understanding to the matter. The commission has not established that this was so, although it did establish clearly that means used by the state and the Church to deal with child sexual abuse in the past were not effective.

What the commission simplistically calls a 'cover-up' as a term of condemnation is in reality far more complex. The commission fails to locate its investigation in the historical context; it also fails to relate it to the management of similar situations by other contemporary organisations and in the context of the complexities of human life, embarrassment and fear and hurt.

Unless the commission's verdict is based on evidence not contained in the report, evidence which we may not see until 2039, when the embargo on disclosing the material ends, its case does not stand.

Naming 'Culprits'

The Murphy Report is outstanding in that it gets so much right, bringing out into the light information about abuse about which there had been rumours for years. This vindicated and gave closure to those who had been abused and whose stories could now be seen to be validated, something that is very welcome.

The report is also striking in that it is so direct, so categorical, so uncompromising in its assessments. This is its dangerous attraction. As well as asserting, in response to the claim of Church officials that, prior to the 1990s, they were on a 'learning curve' in relation to child sexual abuse that it did not 'accept the truth of such claims and assertions' (1.14); as well as having no doubt 'that clerical child sexual abuse was covered up by the archdiocese of Dublin and other Church authorities (1.113); as well as finding that 'the welfare of children, which should have been the first priority, was not even a factor to be considered in the early stages (1.113); and that the McCabe case 'encapsulates everything that was wrong with the archdiocesan handling of child sexual abuse cases'(20.176), the report is uncompromising in its view of the priests of the diocese:

> 1.24: Some priests were aware that particular instances of abuse had occurred. A few were courageous and brought complaints to the attention of their superiors. The vast majority simply chose to turn a blind eye.

How could the commission possibly know this? They provide no evidence whatsoever to justify this allegation. The phrase 'the vast majority' indicates a large number of priests. Did the commission do a survey of diocesan priests? I was not asked, nor was any priest I know asked. The only sense I can make of it is that it came across a number of priests who would fit this description and generalised from that. It had already declared diocesan officials untrustworthy and untruthful: now, by its categorical assertion that 'the vast majority simply chose to turn a blind eye', it effectively blackens, without foundation, the names of a large number of priests of the diocese.

The commission served us well in the matter of establishing stories of abuse. In the matter of failed handling of allegations, however, they seem intent on naming culprits – and the culprits are predominantly on the Church side. They seem not to allow any possibility of situations in which there is no culprit: that the very best of efforts, with the best advice available, will avail nothing. Naming culprits may satisfy anger and bring some comfort to those who were abused but may not always reflect reality. Although it is possible that there are people guilty of dereliction of duty in the handling of the allegations, the report shows that the commission is not the body to name the culprits.

Some will say: 'The Murphy Report names and blames diocesan officials in the handling of allegations. Their very silence in the wake of the report is surely an admission of guilt.' This seems conclusive proof. But there are problems with this, both within the process of the commission and after the report was issued.

It seems that the commission was authorised to attack the good name of citizens, under privilege and protected by provisions of confidentiality accompanied by disproportionate penalties which prevent citizens from defending their good name, not to speak of the prohibitive cost, financial and personal, of seeking to take high court and/or supreme court proceedings.

In view of all these disabling provisions, it is not surprising that those named and blamed in the report would be most reluctant to take the matter further.

There is a common public perception that if bishops resigned they knew they were guilty. Yes, two former auxiliary bishops of Dublin who had transferred to other dioceses tendered their resignations, which were accepted. One former auxiliary who had transferred did not tender his resignation but faced enormous pressure from the media to do so. Two current auxiliary bishops of Dublin tendered their resignations, which were not accepted by Rome (giving rise to media protests). A former archbishop and a former auxiliary bishop had already retired at the time of the publication of *The Murphy Report*. The question of the precise motives of each individual bishop who tendered his resignation is one which can be answered only by them.

It may be the case for any of the bishops that he resigned because he realised that he was guilty of serious dereliction of duty, of lacking in compassion for those who were abused and for their families. It may also be the case for any of the bishops that he resigned because he recognised that, although he understood the serious injury to a child, he let his commitment to the diocese lead him to act to protect the diocese rather than the child, recklessly cover up for the abuser and fail to do his utmost to implement measures to safeguard children.

Alternatively, it may be the case that he honestly thought he did his best, even though he failed to prevent recurring abuse; and that he found the operation of the commission of investigation such a harrowing experience and the launch of *The Murphy Report* and its media aftermath so dreadful that, knowing he now had no future as a bishop, having lost the trust of the people he served, the only rational course of action was to offer his resignation.

After the publication of *The Murphy Report* in 2009 and the media's treatment of the report, the bishops who are 'named and shamed' in the report were perceived as villains, two-dimensional characters. No bishop named in the report has yet made public his account of what happened and the thirty-year embargo means that anyone who gave evidence to the commission is prevented from revealing it. To fill this gap, I offer, in the next chapter, one possible account. I have not asked any of the bishops to write this but perhaps some of it may ring true. If the chapter helps to throw some little light on why some bishops resigned, that will be good.

Some readers may feel that, in giving voice to an imaginary bishop, I am far too kind. This may be so. In that case, all I can say is that this is not the worst criticism I have ever had to deal with. The next chapter is fiction, imagination, although this does not necessarily mean that there is no truth in it.

To provide some balance, I have tried in the following chapter (Chapter 10) to understand what may have gone on in the minds of the members of the commission as they completed the report.

9

Letter from an Imaginary Bishop

'*Dear* _____

I served in this diocese of Dublin as a priest in various appointments. I now serve as an auxiliary bishop. In case anyone thinks this is a very exalted position, I sometimes describe it as being a 'Confirmation machine'! Administering Confirmation around the diocese takes up an enormous amount of time from January to June each year. But enjoyable.

In the course of other work, along with the other bishops of the diocese, I have come across allegations that priests of the diocese were sexually abusing children. Frequently people report it to the diocese, not wanting to approach the Garda about it. We respect that. The stories are disturbing and establishing the facts is difficult. The diocese has a responsibility to anyone abused in this way and also to the priest concerned. We discuss how best to handle these matters and we take psychological, psychiatric and legal advice, while maintaining the confidentiality which seems best for all concerned. There was no protocol here, no agreed procedures, at least not until 1996.

Working in this way, it's inevitable that there will be mistakes but we do our honest best. We are very much aware that even with our very best efforts, with all the professional advice, it seems to make no difference to those who we now know have certainly abused children. The nature of the allegations varies and the number of allegations increases steadily. There were sixteen allegations in the course of the 1960s and 1970s; there were two hundred and forty-six in the course of the 1980s and

1990s. The public and the media are also becoming more aware of these matters, both in the Church and in society. There have been *The Ryan Report* and *The Ferns Report*, as well as the *SAVI* report of 2002 which dealt with sexual assault and violence in Irish society as a whole.

Then the commission of investigation is established. We have considerable apprehension about it, naturally, but at least we feel it will clarify the whole situation. Documents are submitted and I, like others, give evidence before the commission of legal people. We trust that such a commission will act fairly and justly towards all. Since sessions of the commission are in private, we are a bit in the dark about what other submissions there may be, which makes it a bit like walking in a thick haze. How the commission decides whether to accept our submissions and our corrections in order to draft pieces of their report is a bit of a mystery but we hope we can trust them to assess the facts impartially and without any agenda of their own.

We hear that *The Murphy Report* is coming soon and indications seem ominous. Then the report comes and all hell breaks loose. As presented in the media, all of us diocesan officials who were involved in any way in the handling of allegations of child abuse are just downright villains. Our photographs are in the newspapers for all to see. Any word at all which seems to minimise the impact of the report is taken as the Church denying reality all over again and, even worse, interpreted as an attempt to wriggle out of responsibility for the suffering of those who were abused and to deny their experience. To be a person 'named' in *The Murphy Report* is sufficient to be recognised as guilty beyond any doubt whatsoever.

We never anticipated that the commission would turn out to be a trial in all but name in the eyes of the public and the media. We know that our handling of allegations was defective and that in many cases it was utterly futile. If only we had known in the

1970s and 1980s what we understand now about the damage done to children, even into their adulthood, and if we had known the seemingly insurmountable difficulties of dealing with the abusers. But the report denies even that: it tells the world that we knew all along and that, for selfish reasons, we set child abusers loose on the unsuspecting population of the diocese, which covers all of the county of Dublin, most of Wicklow and parts of Kildare, Carlow, Wexford and Laois. The commission tells us they don't believe what we told them. The whole country wants to be rid of us. Immediately. No excuses, please – we just don't want to hear a word from totally discredited people like you! Resign in ignominy. Wear sackcloth and ashes forever. You failed your people, you betrayed your church and your vocation and your faith. You aided and abetted the abuse of innocent children. You have brought shame on your country. Just go.

It's difficult to appear in public. Is there any future for me? What can I do? I could make a court appeal but think what the media would make of that. Even if a court were to rule in my favour, it would be seen as just a legal loophole. In the court of public opinion there is no room for appeal.

Yes, we were concerned about the reputation of the Church – and why not? Did we put this before the welfare of the abused children? Our attention in practice certainly centred around the priest we found was abusing children, rather than on the children. We knew clearly that the abuse was wrong. We thought we should do all in our power to bring about change in him, with the help of professional advice. We tried so many things and so little worked. But our failure to attend to the child was not because we did not care about the child or about the adult who had been abused as a child. The explanation is much more simple. The reason is that at that time nobody was talking about what abuse did to the child. If I understand correctly, it was only in the early 1980s that this began to be addressed in the USA. It was the early 1990s before such awareness was really found in Ireland. Of course we knew that there was abuse but we had no idea of the extent. We knew it was wrong but there were no clear guidelines about what to do, so we had to try in various ways. We knew the priest was committing serious offences; we tried to get him to change but we had no idea how difficult this would be. We knew that it was a serious wrong done to the child; we had no idea how deep or how long-lasting this could be.

I know I've failed many people in this matter but not out of any wilful selfishness. I have failed the people I wanted to dedicate my life to serving. I know people are incredibly angry. Even some people I've worked with for years now want nothing to do with me. If it were not for my family and friends, I'd have nowhere to turn and I even wonder what they think of me. Clearly, my work as a bishop is over. It's the end of the story. The only sensible thing I can do is tender my resignation, in the hope that it will be accepted quickly. I know it will be interpreted by the public as a confession of guilt but there's nothing I can do about that.

Strange though it may seem, there are four sources of consolation in the whole affair.

Firstly, in *The Murphy Report* itself, it is encouraging that in the case of twenty-seven of the forty-five child sexual abuse cases, the commission gives some degree of approval. These cases, of course, received no attention in the media — all the attention was on the other eighteen cases. Nevertheless, we did not get everything wrong, even according to the report.

Secondly, I know that in some cases the commission gets it wrong. It's not politically acceptable to say that at present, of course, but I know it to be the case.

Thirdly, I know that we did manage to offer real help to some of those who were abused and who came to us for support. This does not take away from the experience of those who did not get help — and these are the stories most often heard in the media.

I do not expect those who were helped to come forward; their privacy is most important.

Fourthly, I know that in the case of some abusers, we did help them to turn their lives around to some degree, even though for many, our efforts were in vain. Jesus spoke about it being those who are sick who need the doctor, not those who are well. Whatever the root of the abuse, the Church cannot simply abandon those who go so badly wrong. They are our brothers. Jesus came for them just as much as for the rest of us. I hope that the Church and the nation of which we are citizens will find more and more effective ways of dealing with this terrible blight of child abuse and indeed all kinds of abuse. The learning curve continues.

How do I feel now about the whole affair?

I feel anger at the fact that so many children should have had such injustice and injury inflicted on them. I feel sadness that their Church, our Church, failed them so badly. I feel sadness and anger that there is so much abuse in Irish society and that Church and state continue to fail children.

I feel anger at those who inflicted this abuse on the children and, through the children, on their families. I feel anger and sadness that the abusers were serving in this diocese alongside so many colleagues to whom such abuse is complete anathema.

As regards the officials of the diocese who had responsibility for handling the allegations of abuse, I must first say that I am in no position to declare any one of them innocent or guilty as I simply do not have the necessary facts. But I do feel anger that they have been pilloried in public, without any assessment of the cases in the context of their times and of the knowledge and understanding of the problem as it was then. I feel sadness for those who, the commission declared, were people whose word could not be trusted and who really knew all along, yet recklessly abandoned their responsibilities.

How do I feel about the commission whose task it was to investigate the handling of allegations by Church and state authorities? They had an unenviable task of working through so many stories of suffering for more than three years. They achieved a lot and the report is a milestone in the story of the diocese of Dublin. They gave an authoritative voice to the abused, who had been almost voiceless. But I feel great disappointment that their work is blighted by so many errors and shortcomings.

Perhaps their over-riding difficulty was this: the members of the commission had not themselves had the experience of trying to deal with the allegations, as we had over many years. They had no idea of how difficult it was for us to work out how we could best deal with the situation. If they had listened to us, we could have learned together and worked together. Instead, in the first chapter of the report, they tell us that they just don't believe us and they accuse us of deliberately trying to deceive them. I'm sure that state authorities – the health services, the Gardaí, social welfare, education, justice – must have had just as much difficulty as we did but we don't have enough information about them. There were also non-governmental organisations like the Society for Prevention of Cruelty to Children, boy scouts and girl guides, sports organisations, the Rape Crisis Centre – what did they know? When did they know? What did they do?

There is something very strange about *The Murphy Report*. Priests against whom allegations of abuse had been made and who had faced trial in the courts were named. Those who had not faced trial were give pseudonyms: the report does not explain why but I presume it was so that subsequent legal proceedings would not be prejudiced and the trials could proceed fairly with the necessary safeguards for the accused. But diocesan officials were not given the protection of pseudonyms. We have not been accused of breaking any law. The Murphy Commission was not a court of law. Its standard of proof was not as stringent as would be the case in a criminal or civil action; it was more like the Moriarty Tribunal: 'a reasoned and informed expression of opinion'. Because its assessment is not a verdict but an expression of opinion, the commission had no power to impose a penalty as a court could. But the commission could and did, impose another kind of penalty. Many of us, who did not have the shield of a pseudonym nor the safeguards we would have had in a court, were in effect publicly declared guilty.

In some ways the effects of this are worse than a prison sentence. It is not comparable to the sentence given to those who were abused and who had to endure for so long but still it is a sentence. It gave rise to bishops and other diocesan officials being described in public, individually or collectively, as 'the disgraced bishop (name)'; 'morally bankrupt'; 'devoid of credibility'; 'a totally corrupt institution'.

To be accused of being a collaborator in sexual abuse and rape of children, as we bishops were by Fintan O'Toole in *The Irish Times,* is no less serious than being accused of the abuse or rape itself. We are branded forever as villains of the worst kind. This kind of attack is justified on the basis of 'a reasoned and informed expression of opinion' on the part of the commission and there is no room for any other 'reasoned and informed expression of opinion'. The assessment of the commission of investigation has now become an infallible and unquestionable verdict, not, perhaps, handed down, by the commission itself in those terms but by the court of public opinion. To attempt to put forward an alternative expression of opinion is to have further opprobrium heaped on us, with accusations of being in denial and of denying closure to those who were so unjustly abused and even of inflicting further abuse on them. How did *The Murphy Report* attain this level of unassailability?

There now, I've said it. Those who were abused as children were voiceless for so long. Now we are voiceless. In neither case is it right or just. If what I have written offends you I deeply regret it but I believe I have written only the truth. Nobody should be sentenced to be voiceless or defenceless. An essential part of the mission of the Church is to be, along with others in the world, a voice for the oppressed, the abused, the poor, the marginalised. The Church is certainly not near perfect but if it is rendered voiceless, all of us lose. It has saddened me that since *The Murphy Report,* we Irish Catholic bishops, even in statements we have issued on social justice, seem to have lacked the fire that is so urgently needed.

I feel great disappointment too that the legislation under which the commission was established makes it impossible until 2039 to hear the full story. *The Murphy Report* is not the report that was needed by those who were abused, by the people of Ireland, by the government, or by the diocese of Dublin.

Nevertheless, I am encouraged that the report, whatever its failings, is a milestone of hope that in the coming years the incidence of abuse of children will grow less and less, now that public awareness of the problem has been highlighted and so many people in the diocese are actively involved in the safeguarding of our children. The diocesan updates every year show evidence of this.

For me, little remains. I recognise that nothing I say or do has a chance of being heard or accepted. The only sensible course of action for me now is to send in my resignation.

Yours sincerely
,
_____

10

What Gave Rise to the Failures in *The Murphy Report*?

Various possibilities might be advanced: incompetence; under-resourcing; conspiracy; the commission being fed with false information; prejudice. But, strange as it may seem, I think that the most likely source of the failures in the report is human error.

'People sometimes make errors,' said Dr Edward Weiler., NASA's Associate Administrator for Space Science*. A blinding flash of the obvious. But the error in question cost about $125 million, when the Mars Climate Orbiter spacecraft crashed into the surface of Mars. Two teams worked together. One team used English units (inches, feet, pounds), while the other used metric units. Oops! The craft was launched in December 1998 and lost in September 1999. If someone enquired beforehand whether such a thing could happen, we can imagine the reply: 'Never! We have our systems and our checks. Whatever else might happen, this certainly could not.' But it happened. Simple error; serious outcome.

Likewise, there was human error in Croke Park in Dublin on 18 August 2013 when Galway and Limerick met in the All-Ireland minor hurling semi-final. Hawkeye, the score detection system, showed a false 'miss' when the score was valid. A statement from the Hawkeye company said: 'All the settings were adjusted to cater for hurling, bar one value for the Hill 16 end posts, which was set for football.' Oops! It happened. Simple error: serious outcome.

There are so many examples of error in human endeavour,

* www.mars.jpl.nasa.gov

even errors with very serious consequences that control systems should have uncovered well in advance. To take one example of many, the accomplishments of modern medicine are remarkable. *To Err is Human: Building a Safer Health System* is the title of a 1999 report of the US Institute of Medicine (IOM)[*] An IOM article on the report in November 1999 tells us: 'At least 44,000 people, and perhaps as many as 98,000 people, die in hospitals each year as a result of medical errors that could have been prevented, according to estimates from two major studies.' The article states: '…the majority of medical errors do not result from individual recklessness or the actions of a particular group – this is not a "bad apple" problem. More commonly, errors are caused by faulty systems, processes and conditions that lead people to make mistakes or fail to prevent them.'

To dismiss the possibilities of serious error in any endeavour involving human beings, including the Church and the law, is as rash as providing insufficient lifeboats on the *Titanic.* Disaster can so easily strike.

With the Murphy Commission, I can only conjecture. But, based on the report of the commission, I suggest a hypothesis. I cannot verify it and I offer it simply as a possible scenario.

I have no information about what went on in the minds of the members of the commission, except, again, for their report. We do know what Archbishop Diarmuid Martin said, in a TV3 broadcast, about his own state of mind on reading the files. It was on 16 June 2009, around the time the report was to be sent to the minister:

'One weekend I decided to try and get through these documents. I came to the stage when I simply threw them onto the ground. I couldn't keep reading. This is reality. It can't be hidden and it shouldn't be hidden.'

If this was his reaction, what was it like for members of

---

[*]   www.iom.edu

the commission who had the task of studying the documents for three long years? The horrors of the abuse inflicted on so many children must have been close to soul-destroying. Between reading and discussing the documents and interviewing people who were involved in the handling of allegations it was a very difficult task.

I offer my hypothesis in the form of a short dramatisation, condensing the processes of three years' work into a few paragraphs.

'This is outrageous! What those men did to all those children! Surely nobody would do that to a child. It's almost unimaginable! How on earth could men whose lives were supposed to be dedicated totally to enhancing the lives of others, including children – how could those priests have ever come to this?'

'How is it that those men were set loose on trusting children? Was there no control over them? Who sent them? Did anyone ever think that they should be monitored? At the very first whiff of any suspicion or allegation, they should have been removed totally from all possibility of doing any more damage!'

'Who was responsible for them? Why did they not do their job? They've been in business for 2000 years – they should have known what to do. They must have known what to do! They can have no possible excuses. They cannot deny it. We cannot let them deny it. They cannot escape their responsibilities!'

'Why were those men who abused the children not brought to justice right away? We cannot do anything about that – our mandate is not to investigate those who abused the children but those who were supposed to deal effectively with the allegations. We even have to use pseudonyms for those abusers who have not yet been brought to court.'

'This disgraceful duplicity, this total dereliction of duty on the part of the diocese – this must be exposed! For the sake of the children, for the sake of their families, for the sake of the country, it must all be exposed. No holding back!'

'We are a commission of investigation; we are not a court of law. We

have no power to impose any penalties. What can we do in this horrifying matter? The very least we can do is to name those who were responsible for the priests who abused and supposed to be responsible for protecting and caring for the children. The best we can do is to let the whole country know about it, without any ambiguity of language. It just has to come out. We can do that in our report for all to see.'

It's a short step from sentiments like this to the report we have. My scenario may have elements of caricature, as it condenses a long process into a few lines. It is not designed in any sense to belittle the work of the commission; rather, it is a recognition of some of the difficulties they faced. Furthermore, I can write it only because that is the way my own mind might have worked if I were a member of the commission.

If my hypothesis in some way resembles reality and even if the members of the commission were not overtly aware that this is how it was, they produced the report as we have it, for the best of reasons as they saw it. They gave voice to many who were abused and we must not undervalue this.

But by denying the facts of very recent history and failing to place their narrative in the context of sexual abuse of children in Irish society or relating it in some way to how such abuse is handled by other authorities in Irish society, they missed the mark.

Being a member of a commission of investigation, or a judge or barrister or solicitor, does not mean relinquishing our human nature. It means being all the more aware of and sensitive to human nature, to how people live their lives. Members of the legal profession are people too – just like the children who were abused. And indeed, just like bishops and other diocesan officials.

If I disagree with the Murphy Commission, do I show a lack of respect? When Archbishop Diarmuid Martin gave the Russo Family Lecture in Fordham on 24 April 2013, he confessed: 'When I was asked to return to Dublin, Pope John Paul asked me why secularisation had taken place so rapidly in Ireland. It was one of the rare occasions when I told a Pope he was wrong!' It does not show respect to voice agreement or simply remain silent when you believe that those you address are wrong. The greatest respect is honesty.

The Murphy Commission told many diocesan officials that they were wrong. I now say that the commission was wrong in many ways. My wish is that this book should bring about a debate. If *The Murphy Report* contains errors, I am sure that the commission would wish these to be examined and addressed. They would not want to be remembered for perpetuating error or injustice.

Those dealing with allegations of child sexual abuse in the 1960s and 1970s and 1980s did so by trial and error. They had no previous knowledge of how to go. Staying still was not an option. They had no street map, compass, or GPS and there were no familiar landmarks to indicate whether they were on the right road. They were in the fog. Of course they went wrong. Frequently they did not arrive at the destination they wanted and that we would want. Sadly, they were unable to find the protection the children needed or the way to bring the abusers back to the right path. But they looked for guidance and they tried.

The Catholic Church in Ireland has put in place many effective measures to prevent a recurrence of the failures of the past; *The Murphy Report* and other such reports have helped the Church in this in no small way.

It remains to be seen how errors in the work of the Murphy Commission are acknowledged, investigated and dealt with effectively to prevent such errors happening again.

11

Conclusion

Sexual abuse of children (or of any person) is a totally reprehensible act. It brings serious consequences for an abused
person. Such abuse is widespread in human society, not just in
Ireland. *The Murphy Report* provides valuable documentation of
its occurrence as perpetrated by clergy serving in the diocese of
Dublin and, although its mandate did not include a study of the
abuse itself, documenting some of the abuse has served a vital
function in validating the stories of those who were abused and
who reported allegations of this to Church and state.

The mandate of the Murphy Commission was to investigate
how allegations were handled by Church and state authorities.
In the presentation and interpretation of how allegations were
handled and in its assessments of these matters, the commission
has failed in so many ways that it is not a reliable guide. It fails
seriously when it does not take into account the historical realities
of the times and the practices of other authorities in managing
such allegations or place the investigation in the context of child
sexual abuse in Irish society today.

Of course mistakes were made in the handling of allegations
of child sexual abuse. But in denying the 'learning curve' and in
assigning deceitful and selfish motives to Church authorities, the
commission makes serious unsubstantiated allegations against
many people who have been seriously affected by its assessments.
To blame Church authorities for failing to take into account the
welfare of children in this matter, at a time when the effects of
sexual abuse on children was little understood, is unwarranted.

This is not to imply that children did not suffer grievous injustice or that Church authorities were in no way culpable at any time. Nor is it to imply that the reputation of the Church was not an important consideration to these authorities.

If what I have written in this book is true, it is important that remedial action be taken. This is not a matter of compensation, as the destruction of a person's reputation cannot be mended in any monetary way. That damage done by the report is not something we can compare to the damage done to children who are sexually abused. Both, however, are matters of justice. Both must be addressed.

The Murphy Report was forwarded to the appropriate minister on 21 July 2009. It was published on 26 November 2009. In those four months, the report was examined closely and decisions were made about parts to be 'redacted' – omitted for legal reasons – until legal proceedings were finished. Over this period, is it possible that no person in the department raised a question about the many errors in the report? Did they find all the needles in the haystack and overlook several large anchors?

There are very competent investigative journalists in Ireland. Since the publication of the report, is it possible that not a single journalist had misgivings about the report? This book is the limited attempt of one person to evaluate *The Murphy Report*.

No doubt it will be said that I am highly presumptuous to publish a book such as this. I fully acknowledge that I have no standing in the matter and that my only qualification is that I am a citizen of this country. Whether this book is of any value has to depend on the truth of what it contains. On this and on no other grounds do I offer it. The verdict must rest with those who examine what I have written, just as I have attempted to examine what is written in *The Murphy Report*.

Areas which require further study may be:

- The relationship between the Canon Law of the Church and the civil law of the state
- The developments in thinking behind Canon Law and civil law
- The developments in psychiatric and psychological understanding of child sexual abuse victims and abusers and in the possible treatments for abusers
- The sociological understanding of how this country has reacted to reports of child sexual abuse in society and in the Church and how society may find comfort in dealing with this kind of problem by focusing on a particular group within society

The Commissions of Investigation Act 2004, under which the government established the Murphy Commission, also needs to be re-examined

When people face unprecedented situations without sufficient data or understanding, it is inevitable that there will be failures. Church and state can learn from each other and work together, as, thankfully, has now become more common. Castigating or blaming the other, or attributing base motives to the other, or rejecting without foundation what the other asserts is certainly not what is needed. Horror and anger at the awful reality of child sexual abuse provide a driving force for change. What we need is described in a saying attributed to St Augustine of Hippo: 'Hope has two beautiful daughters. Their names are anger and courage: anger at the way things are and courage to see that they do not remain the way they are.'

Bibliography

Books, Journals, Articles and Blogs

Breen, Michael. 'Through the Looking Glass: How the Mass Media Represent, Reflect and Refract Sexual Crime in Ireland.' *Irish Communications Review*, 10, 2007, pp. 5-22. www.dit.ie.

Buckley, Helen, Caroline Skehill and Eoin O'Sullivan. *Child Protection Practices in Ireland: A Case Study.* Oak Tree Press, 1997. hse.openrepository. com.

Buckley, Helen. *ChildLinks* (11). Barnardos. www.barnardos.ie.

Cling, B.J. *Sexualized Violence Against Women and Children: A Psychology and Law Perspective.* Guilford Press, 2004.

Furrow, The: A Journal for the Contemporary Church. St Patrick's College, Maynooth.

Keenan, Marie. *Child Sexual Abuse and the Catholic Church.* Oxford, 2012.

Kundera, Milan. *Testaments Betrayed: An Essay in Nine Parts.* Harper Perennial, 1993.

McKeown, Kieran and Robbie Gilligan. *Economic and Social Review*, January 1991. www.tara.tcd.ie.

Paolucci, E. O., M. L. Genuis and C. Violato. 'A Meta-analysis of the Published Research on the Effects of Child Sexual Abuse.' *The Journal of Psychology: Interdisciplinary and Applied*, 135, 1, 2001. National Foundation for Family Research and Education, Calgary. www.tandfonline.com.

Wynne, Jane. 'Flamingos or Sparrows,' in Richardson, S. and H. Bacon. *Creative Responses to Child Sexual Abuse.* Jessica Kingsley Publishers, 2003.

Shakeshaft, Charol. *Educator Sexual Misconduct: A Synthesis of Existing Literature.* US Department of Education, 2004.

Sweeney, Fergal. *Commissions of Investigation and Procedural Fairness: A Review from a Legal Perspective of The Murphy Report.* Association of Catholic Priests, October 2013.

thethirstygargoyle.blogspot.com

Reports and Policy Documents

Catholic Youth Ministry Ireland. *Safeguarding Children: Standards and Guidance Document for the Catholic Church in Ireland.* Maynooth, 2009. www.cymi.ie.

Children Acts Advisory Board. *Report of an Audit of Child Protection Research in Ireland 1990-2009.* www.tara.tcd.ie.

Commissions of Investigation Act, 2004: www.irishstatutebook.ie.

Church of Ireland [Anglican Communion] 1997. *Safeguarding Trust.* www.ireland.anglican.org.

Church of England. *Responding Well to Those Who Have Been Sexually Abused* 2011. www.churchofengland.org.

Deetman Commission Report (Onderzoekscommissie) into Child Sexual Abuse in the Catholic Church, December 2011. www.onderzoekrk.nl.

Department of Health. *Memorandum on Non-Accidental Injuries to Children* March 1977 and 1987 edition. www.lenus.ie.

Department of Children and Youth Affairs. *Children First: National Guidance for the Protection and Welfare of Children,* 2011. www.hse.ie.

Dublin Diocesan *Child Protection Update,* 30 May 2013. www.dublindiocese.ie.

Dublin Diocesan *Child Protection Newsletter,* Autumn 2012. www.csps.dublindiocese.ie.

Dublin Rape Crisis Centre *Annual Reports:* www.drcc.ie.

Dublin Rape Crisis Centre. *Sexual Abuse and Violence in Ireland (SAVI):* Report by McGee, H., J. Byrne, R. Conroy, M. de Barra, R. Garavan. Royal College of Surgeons, 2002. www.drcc.ie or www.epubs.rcsi.ie.

Dublin Rape Crisis Centre. *SAVI Revisited* (2005). www.drcc.ie.

Eastern Health Board. *The Dublin Rape Crisis Centre: A Process Evaluation.* October 1989. www.lenus.ie.

The Ferns Report: Government Publications. www.ferns.ie.

An Garda Síochána: *Recent Rape/Sexual Assault: National Guidelines on Referral and Forensic Clinical Examination in Ireland.* 2010.

Garda Inspectorate. *Responding to Child Sexual Abuse.* 2012.

Health Services Executive. *Child Protection and Welfare Practice Handbook,* 2011: www.hse.ie.

Irish Catholic Bishops' Advisory Committee. *Child Sexual Abuse: Framework for a Church Response,* 1996. www.catholicbishops.ie.

Methodist Church in Ireland (in conjunction with the Presbyterian Board of Social Witness). *Taking Care.* www.irishmethodist.org.

The Murphy Report: Department of Justice. www.justice.ie.

Presbyterian Church in Ireland. *Taking Care Two,* 2011. www.presbyterianireland.org.

Press Council of Ireland: *Publication Guidelines for Newspapers and Magazines.*

Appendix I: Summary Table of the Forty-six Cases

Details of the forty-six cases investigated by the commission appear in *The Murphy Report*, taking up 462 pages. The information given by the commission varies from case to case, depending on what it was able to establish. In the Assessment column, I give, where possible, a short phrase directly from the commission's assessment; otherwise, I give my own summary of what the commission says.

Media coverage of the report may have helped create an impression that the report is a catalogue of unrelieved disaster. In fact:

- In twenty-seven cases, diocesan handling receives approval from the commission in varying degrees.
- In eighteen cases, diocesan handling receives criticism from the commission in varying degrees.

The remaining case (Chapter 49) involved inappropriate behaviour rather than abuse.

Abbreviations
*=pseudonym
D=diocese/R=religious order or congregation
O=order or congregation (in Commission's Assessment column)
CSA=child sexual abuse
CPS=Child Protection Service of Dublin Archdiocese
G=Garda
HB=Health Board or HSE
SW=social worker

Ch.	Name	P.	Status	First Complaint	Commission's Assessment of Diocese and/or Order	D Bad?	Commission's Assessment of State Authorities
12	Fr James McNamee	177	D	1960	More concerned with scandal	X	G helpful
13	Fr Edmondus*	188	D	1960	Very badly handled	X	G failed at first. HB mixed
14	Fr Phineas*	210	D	2005	Allegations unclear. Dealt properly		
15	Fr Vidal *	212	UK	1973	Not a good news story	X	
16	Fr Patrick Maguire	217	R	1974	Very badly handled by Society and diocese	X	G and HB acted appropriately
17	Fr Ioannes*	239	D	1974	Quite simply disastrous	X	G dealt well 1994; badly 1995
18	Fr Tyrus*	250	D		Grave concerns	X	No evidence of criminal behaviour
19	Fr Tony Walsh	252	D	1978	Action should have been taken at a much earlier stage	X	G unacceptable
20	Fr Patrick McCabe	282	D	1977	Encapsulates everything that was wrong	X	G failed
21	Fr Horatio*	344	D	1980	Blind eye / dealt appropriately		Connivance by Garda is shocking
22	Fr Donal Gallagher	353	R	1981	O failed; diocese not told		G shortcomings. SW acted appropriately
23	Fr Hugo*	360	D	1981	D failed	X	G files no record
24	Fr Ivan Payne	363	D	1981	Handled very badly	X	G dealt appropriately
25	Fr Donato*	386	D	1995	PP did not tell diocese	X	G acted appropriately

Ch.	Name	P.	Status	First Complaint	Commission's Assessment of Diocese and/or Order	D Bad?	Commission's Assessment of State Authorities
26	Fr Harry Moore	390	D	1982	Totally inadequate	X	G acted appropriately
27	Fr Septimus*	400	D	1982	Inadequate	X	
28	Fr William Carney	414	D	1983	Nothing short of catastrophic	X	HB failed. G efficient
29	Fr Thomas Naughton	455	R-D	1983	Very poor handling; belatedly acted correctly	X	G and HB acted well
30	Fr Cicero*	470	Ossory	1986	Mixed		
31	Fr Clemens*	478	D	1988	Dealt quite well		
32	Fr Dominic S Boland	482	R	1989	O relatively good for 1989		G appropriately
33	Fr Quinton*	494	R	1991	D was correct		HB should have notified G
34	Fr Marius*	506	D	92	Delays; no monitoring	X	
35	Fr Noel Reynolds	514	D	1994	Extremely badly handled	X	G thorough investigation. HB not involved
36	Fr Daryus*	529	D	1960s; 1994	Effective		
37	Fr Terentius*	532	R	1994	O dealt well		No complaint to G
38	Fr John Kinsella	544	UK-D	1995	D no jurisdiction but acted well		G effective
39	Fr Laurentius*	547	R	(1990) 1995	O acted well, diocese not told		G acted appropriately
40	Fr Klaudius*	558	R	1995	O delayed report to HB, diocese not told		HB should have notified schools and Dept. Ed.
41	Fr Francis McCarthy	565	D	1995	D and State acted well together		
42	Fr Sergius*	575	D	95	D failed	X	G acted appropriately
43	Fr Dante*	581	D	1995	D acted appropriately		G acted appropriately

Ch.	Name	P.	Status	First Complaint	Commission's Assessment of Diocese and/or Order	D Bad?	Commission's Assessment of State Authorities
44	Fr Cassius*	590	D	1999	Old complaint: D did what they could.		Old complaint: G did what they could.
45	Fr Giraldus*	592	R-D	2000	Procedural difficulties. D facilitated complainant		HSE late with documents
46	Fr Aquila*	598	R	2000	O and D acted appropriately		G acted appropriately
47	Fr Blaise*	601	D	2001	Possible mistaken identity. D acted well		G assisted complainant
48	Fr Benito*	603	D	2001	D acted well; some confusion. CPS acted well		G acted appropriately
49	Fr Magnus*	611	D	2001?	Inappropriate behaviour		
50	Fr Jacobus*	613	R	2002	Conflicting versions; allegation withdrawn. O and D acted well		Complainant did not cooperate with G
51	Fr Guido*	617	D	2002	Inappropriate behaviour. D acted correctly		
52	Fr Rufus *	621	D	2002	Difficult case. D acted properly		
53	Fr Ignatio *	626	R	2002	Probable mistaken identity. O acted well		G acted appropriately
54	Fr Cornelius *	629	D	2002	Inappropriate behaviour. D dealt appropriately		G dealt appropriately
55	Fr Ricardus *	631	D	2003	False allegation. D dealt appropriately		G dealt appropriately
56	Fr Augustus *	635	D	2003	Not CSA. D dealt appropriately		G dealt appropriately
57	Fr Ezio*	637	R	2002	No meaningful investigation possible; O dealt appropriately		G dealt appropriately

Appendix II: Dublin Diocese Child Protection

Dublin Diocesan Child Protection Update, 30 May 2013
A further nine hundred people participated in training and information sessions for the safeguarding of children in the archdiocese of Dublin.

The number of priests, bishops, parish workers, diocesan staff and ancillary staff in schools who have participated in Garda vetting increased by 6300 to 32,600.

No allegation of child abuse was reported against a priest of the archdiocese who was not already the subject of a complaint. The total number of priests against whom an allegation of child sexual abuse has been recorded remains at ninety-eight. This relates to a period of over seventy years.

In the past twelve months a suspicion of child abuse was raised against two priests (one deceased) of the archdiocese who were not previously the subject of complaints.

Two hundred and sixteen civil actions have been taken against forty-nine priests and former priests of the archdiocese. One hundred and sixty-one have been concluded and fifty-five are ongoing.

The costs, so far, to the archdiocese of settlement of claims regarding child sexual abuse by priests is currently at €17.9 million (€12.5 million in settlements and €5.4 million in legal costs for both sides).

Eleven priests or former priests of the archdiocese have been convicted in the criminal courts.

Extract from *Dublin Diocesan Child Protection Newsletter,* Autumn 2012

'The commission is satisfied that there are effective structures and procedures currently in operation.' (*The Murphy Report,* p. 4, section 1.16). Some media coverage of these issues can cause confusion in people's minds because there is often a failure to distinguish between how child protection matters were dealt with before the introduction of the first set of Church guidelines in 1996 and what has happened since then.

When evidence is found of failure to deal adequately with child protection concerns in the pre-1996 period this is often presented as though it demonstrates that the Church failed to comply with its own guidelines. We should not minimise the failures of the past and the often horrific consequences of such failures. Neither should we ignore the fact that there have been situations where Church guidelines have not been followed.

However, the interests of the safety and welfare of children are not well served when the progress that has been made is not acknowledged. It takes considerable courage for people to come forward and to disclose that they were abused by a priest or religious. Many did so because they were determined that other children should not suffer as they did. There have been major advances in the safeguarding and protection of children involved in Church activities in the diocese of Dublin, as in many other dioceses. This was noted by a statutory enquiry and confirmed by the state's own child-protection service. That is a significant vindication of the courageous insistence of the survivors that their stories be heard.

Appendix III: Working towards Healing

The Towards Healing Counselling and Support Services are provided by the Catholic Church in Ireland for survivors of institutional, clerical and religious abuse. The services provided by Towards Healing will be developed in consultation with representatives of survivors. The information in this chapter has been provided by Towards Healing.

Background to the Establishment of the Service
The Towards Healing Counselling and Support Services began on 1 February 2011. This new service replaced the Faoiseamh Counselling Service which had provided counselling to survivors of clerical, religious and institutional abuse since its establishment in 1996. It was set up initially by the Sisters of Mercy in 1996 and then by the executive of the Conference of Religious in Ireland (CORI) to provide support to people who had suffered physical, sexual or emotional abuse in a religious or diocesan setting.

In 2007, the board of directors of Faoiseamh carried out an evaluation of the service and the outcome of this evaluation prompted an extensive process of consultation about future needs of survivors and how these should be met. The process of consultation was undertaken during 2009 and 2010 by the Irish Episcopal Conference (IEC), CORI, the Irish Missionary Union (IMU) and Faoiseamh. It involved meeting survivors of abuse, survivor groups and services, the relevant statutory authorities (the HSE and Gardaí) and individual congregations and dioceses, discussions with experts in other jurisdictions and the analysis of best practice internationally.

The outcome of the consultation was unanimous agreement

that a single Catholic Church response towards meeting the needs of survivors was needed and that such a response needed to be broader than counselling, towards meeting the support needs of survivors on a more holistic basis than heretofore.

Meeting the Support Needs of Survivors

In the light of the extensive consultation and analyses undertaken, Towards Healing provides a wide range of services for survivors, as follows:

- Helpline support and referral
- Face-to-face counselling
- Group work
- Practical workshops
- Friendly call
- Restorative justice/facilitated listening meetings
- Advocacy

All services are provided free of charge.

Client Pathway of Care

The initial point of contact with the service is through the helpline. A person who wishes to receive support phones the helpline and speaks to one of the helpline counsellors/case managers. The person is supported by the helpline counsellor and, if he/she needs face-to-face counselling, is put in contact with a therapist, within a week to ten days. The client can progress through the other services available and, through the continuum of care provided through this range of Towards Healing services, ideally address their individual needs and exit the service altogether.

Face-to-face counselling is offered for up to eighty sessions, over a two-year period, on the basis of one session each week. In the event that a client might need additional support from time to time, this would be provided by the helpline. Counsellors/case managers review the progress of individual clients, in consultation with their therapists and with the clients themselves, at regular intervals i.e. at six, thirty, fifty and seventy sessions, respectively.

When a client reaches sixty sessions their case is reviewed by an external independent review panel which recommends the additional support needed in individual cases. In this context, about 12 per cent of clients require counselling beyond the norm. On the other hand, most clients complete their counselling after forty sessions. It is, of course, open to a client who finishes their therapy to re-register at a future date, if they so wish.

Therapeutic group work has been provided in addition to individual face-to-face counselling and has been found by those attending to be of benefit to them. Equally, practical workshops on matters such as self-care, parenting, anger management are being expanded to address the needs of our clients.

Under the restorative justice/facilitated listening service, survivors are consulted about their objectives and aspirations in meeting with the representatives of the diocese or of the congregation/institution in which their abuse took place, towards enabling them to move on with their lives. The framework for the restorative justice service was developed in consultation with Dr Janine Geske, former supreme court judge of Wisconsin, State of Illinois, USA and currently Professor of Law at the University of Marquette, Illinois, USA.

The friendly call service is designed to offer daily telephone support to clients of Towards Healing as part of their continuum of care.

The advocacy service is designed to link our clients to the broader network of statutory and non-statutory services, such as the HSE, and towards facilitating them in accessing services, other than those provided by Towards Healing, which are appropriate to their needs.

These include general medical and dental services, pension entitlements, housing and finance, psychiatry and addiction services.

Statistics

Since 1996, when the *Faoiseamh* service commenced, a total of 5000 clients have registered with both the Towards Healing and Faoiseamh services. During the period 1996-2012 a total of 316,358 counselling sessions was provided to clients.

The service has experienced peaks in demand following publication of high-profile reports into clerical and religious abuse, notably following the publications of the Ferns, Ryan and Murphy reports. There has been no noticeable decline in overall demand, with the trend being upwards in the number of counselling sessions provided in recent years. In 2010 a total of 25,561 sessions were provided, in 2011 a total of 28,079 and in 2012 a total of 29,261. During 2013, the service is projecting a rise in sessions to 31,000 approximately. When this upward trend is taken together with the fact that 80 per cent of clients who register have never registered with the service in the past, the question of a level of unmet need existing for the service is apparent.

The Financing of the Service

The Towards Healing service is funded jointly by the Irish Episcopal Conference and the Conference of Religious of Ireland/Irish Missionary Union, on a fifty-fifty basis, reflecting the single Catholic Church response which underpins the service. Prior to the establishment of Towards Healing in February 2011, the Faoiseamh Service was funded simply on the basis of the retrospective recoupment of actual costs incurred by individual congregations and dioceses.

The service costs about €2.8 million per annum and the

investment by the Catholic Church in support of the needs of survivors is reflected in the fact that almost €30 million will have been provided by the religious congregations and dioceses by the end of 2013.

Accessing the Service

The Towards Healing service can be accessed by calling the helpline:

Freephone (Ireland): 1800-30316

Freephone (UK and Northern Ireland): 0800-0963315

www.towardshealing.ie

Mobile number for texting for our hearing-impaired service users: 085-8022859

The helpline opening hours are: Monday-Thursday 11am-8.00pm; Friday 11am-6.00pm.

Outside these hours, callers may leave a message on the answering machine and they will be contacted the following day or, in the case of calls left late on a Friday or on a Saturday or Sunday, they will receive a call back on the following Monday.

Appendix IV: '*The Murphy Report*: A Personal Assessment'*

The Murphy Report of the commission of investigation into the handling of allegations of child sexual abuse by priests in the diocese of Dublin 1975-2004 seemed to hit the diocese and the country like a runaway train. A reaction of outrage is very understandable. I have been angry at the long-lasting suffering of those abused as children, whether by clergy or by others. I have been angry at the failures in the way complaints were received and handled by the diocese and at the consequent suffering caused. I feel shamed in the abuse perpetrated by priests with whom I serve in the diocese and by the failures by diocesan authorities in acting in an effective pastoral way. However marginally, I am part of that abusive structure. For those reasons, I welcome the publication of the report.

What I Find Valuable in *The Murphy Report*
We have lived for so many years with rumours and partial truth. This has been particularly difficult for those who were abused. Now we can deal with reality on a firmer basis of fact. *The Murphy Report* documents both effective action and failures on part of church (Dublin diocese and, where applicable, religious order or congregation) and state (Gardaí, health board). The commission has done valuable service to those who were abused, to the people of this country and in particular to all the members of the Catholic Church in Ireland. Putting the protection of ordained priests before the protection and service of lay members of the Church is an injustice. Those people who were abused and

---

* Published in *The Furrow*, February 2010

betrayed and who persisted in challenging the diocese until at last the matter could not be avoided have done the Church a great service. So also have those in the media who supported this challenge.

Truth, we hope, brings justice and new life to those abused. For the Church, it impels us towards the end of Church as empire and towards its true nature of the body of Christ: a communion of people, a community of service, a place of reconciliation. That has never been lost but it has been overshadowed in recent history by a tendency to adopt the model of domination that we find so much in our world. A Church which has lost awareness of its own brokenness is a Church that has lost the ability to serve. Abuse of children was carried out by ordained priests, whose vocation is to encourage and enable respect and reverence for every human being and to serve all the baptised in the living of their priesthood. This is a shattering betrayal, as great an abomination as the abuse of children by a parent, the very person to whom the child should be able to turn to for protection. My prayer is that the present focus on the wrong done by priests will serve also to protect children, and indeed every human being, from abuse in whatever circumstances. We have learned in recent decades that abuse of children, sexual and otherwise, is far more widespread in society than there was any previous awareness of, except on the part of those abused. This shameful episode in the Church could be a lightning rod to serve to protect the human race at large.

Media coverage may have given the impression that the report is a catalogue of unrelieved disaster. It is good to be aware, therefore, that of the forty-five cases about which the report gives an assessment, handling by the Church in twenty-five cases receives some sort of approval from the commission; twenty cases receive varying degrees of criticism. (See Appendix I)

Since appropriate sections of the report were sent, prior to publication, to those whose names were mentioned in it for checking for factual errors, I take it that the historical facts of what occurred are accurate. It must have been a very difficult task for the members of the commission to live with these facts for over three years. The commission drew conclusions from these facts. It is in the area of those conclusions that I would like to raise some questions.

What Right Have I to Assess the Report?

I have found a kind of gut reaction, where the words and the tone of voice say: 'How dare you do anything which would take away from the recognition which the people who were abused have finally achieved after much effort and suffering! How dare you do anything which would let the perpetrators of the abuse off the hook, or which would exonerate the diocesan authorities who so badly failed those abused people!' That is not my intention in what I write here. But in our sense of outrage it is important that we do not lose our capacity for rational thought. I find it extraordinary that I have found not one journalist or commentator who has done the kind of review of the report which would otherwise be normal. The commission, I am sure, would not wish to be burdened with any claim to infallibility. We must not make the report the final and absolute word. There was a Latin saying: '*Roma locuta est – causa finita est!*' – 'Rome has spoken – the case is closed!' It would not be wise to turn that into '*Murphy locuta est…!*'

We cannot afford to have unrealistic expectations of what the Church or the justice system of the country can achieve. The abuse of children is very secretive, whoever the abuser is. Abusers can be highly manipulative. There can be no guarantee that each and every person who was abused will be fully satisfied, or even satisfied at all, with the outcome of proceedings. We know well that our human systems have their limitations and their failures.

Law, however admirable, is administered by human beings.

If you are angry at what I write here, I ask only this: Please read what I write and ask whether it is true. If you judge what I say to be false, please discard it. Even better, try to put into words why you say it is wrong and let me, or the editor of *The Furrow*, know. This debate is overdue.

The Murphy Report in the Context of Irish Society

The Dublin Archdiocese Commission of Investigation was established to report on the handling by Church and state authorities of a representative sample of allegations and suspicions of child sexual abuse against clerics operating under the aegis of the archdiocese of Dublin over the period 1975 to 2004 (Par. 1.1). The commission received over 70,000 documents from the diocese in relation to this enquiry (2.18). If all these documents are relevant to the thirty years, this is an average of more than six documents for each and every day of those thirty years. Even if some of these were of marginal value, it is still a staggering quantity of documentation.

In the case of the Health Services Executive (HSE), the commission was told that, because the HSE files were filed by reference to the name of the abused and were not in any way cross-referenced to the alleged abuser, it would have to examine individually up to 180,000 files in order to ascertain whether an alleged abuser was a priest in the Dublin Archdiocese (2.19). The report remarks: 'The health boards and the HSE do not properly record cases of clerical child sexual abuse (1.98).'

> The Garda Síochána gave what documentation they had. This documentation was quite extensive for the period after 1995. They were unable to supply files in relation to some of their activities in the 1960s, 1970s, or 1980s as these had been destroyed or mislaid. (2.19)

It may be the case that the work of the Murphy Commission was made easier because the diocese kept such full records. If HSE, Garda and other records are not of equal standard, it may indicate, paradoxically, that the diocese, however faulty, had a greater sense of pastoral responsibility for the abused person and for the abuser. For the fullest possible protection of children, an investigation no less thorough needs to be carried out in these other spheres. Will it take another series of media exposures to urge our government into action here?

The findings of the *SAVI* (*Sexual Abuse and Violence in Ireland*) report (2002) are that 'clerical/religious ministers or clerical/religious teachers constituted 3.2 per cent of abusers'. The other 96.8 per cent of abusers are non-clerical. We hear little about how such cases were managed by the relevant bodies. Is it likely that only the diocese managed cases badly? Although not within the remit of the Murphy Commission, it seems important that the records of the HSE, Gardaí and other organisations that have dealings with children also be examined, so that we know whether the same pattern of concealment and protection is to be found there. Otherwise we could presume without foundation that what was done in Dublin diocese was significantly worse than what was done in the rest of society.

How Widespread Was Abuse of Children by Clergy in the Diocese of Dublin?
The Murphy Report states:

> It is abundantly clear, from the commission's investigation as revealed in the cases of the 46 priests in the representative sample (see Chapters 11 to 57), that child sexual abuse by clerics was widespread throughout the period under review. (1.7)
>
> The volume of revelations of child sexual abuse by clergy over the past thirty-five years or so has been described by a Church source as

a 'tsunami' of sexual abuse. He went on to describe the 'tsunami' as 'an earthquake deep beneath the surface hidden from view'. (1.14)

Without doubt, even one crime of child sexual abuse is an abomination. The statistics published by the diocese on 26 November 2009 put the 'tsunami' image in perspective. *The Murphy Report* covers the period 1975 to 2004 and takes a representative sample of forty-six cases out of a total of 172 named priests and eleven unnamed priests, some or all of whom may be included in the one hundred and seventy-two named priests.(1.8) The November 2009 statistics cover the longer period from 1940 to 2009. In this period, about 2800 diocesan and religious priests served in the diocese. Allegations have been made against eighty-four priests of the diocese and sixty religious priests – a total of 144, or about 5 per cent of the total. Not all allegations are later proven true. Ten Dublin priests or former priests have been convicted or have cases pending. Two non-diocesan priests who served in Dublin have been convicted.

The harm that can be done by even one perpetrator to one child is indeed like a tsunami for that child in its consequences but to say that 'child sexual abuse by clerics was widespread throughout the period under review'(1.7) does not accord with the facts. If there were allegations against 5 per cent of teachers, they would rightly protest were this to be described in an official report as 'widespread abuse'.

Were the Priests of the Diocese Complicit in the Concealment of abuse?

Some priests were aware that particular instances of abuse had occurred. A few were courageous and brought complaints to the attention of their superiors. The vast majority simply chose to turn a blind eye. (1.24)

The report does not specify what 'some' means. The phrase 'vast majority' might seem to imply that the number is very large. However, it could mean, for example, that seventy (some) priests were aware of instances; only nine were courageous and sixty-one (the vast majority) turned a blind eye. It could also mean that eleven (some) were aware and that eight (the vast majority) turned a blind eye. The report does not offer precision in this.

It appears that the editorial of *The Irish Times* of 27 November, the day following publication of the report, may have derived from this paragraph. It stated: 'The vast majority of uninvolved priests turned a blind eye.' The context of 'some priests were aware' was not supplied. The editorial therefore alleges that the vast majority of the priests of the diocese were aware of the abuse as they could not be said to turn a blind eye unless they were aware. In its 'Corrections and Clarifications' section on 16 December, *The Irish Times* stated in relation to the editorial: 'This related to those priests who were aware that particular instances of abuse had occurred.' This is neither a correction nor a clarification, since it merely states what was already implied in the editorial. It does not alleviate the seriousness of the allegation, nor does it reduce the scope of the people against whom the allegation was made. In this, *The Irish Times* does not serve the truth well; nor does it do justice to *The Murphy Report*.

How Did Diocesan Authorities Develop over the Review Period?

The report states:

Officials of the archdiocese of Dublin and other Church authorities have repeatedly claimed to have been, prior to the late 1990s, on 'a learning curve' in relation to the matter. Having completed its investigation, the commission does not accept the truth of such claims and assertions. (1.14)

The report continues:

> The claim that bishops and senior church officials were on 'a learning curve' about child sexual abuse rings hollow when it is clear that cases were dealt with by Archbishop McQuaid in the 1950s and 1960s and that, although the majority of complaints emerged from 1995 onwards, many of the complaints described in this report first came to the attention of the archdiocese in the 1970s and 1980s. (1.19)

'Many of the complaints' here, as can be seen from the table above, is eighteen out of forty-six. The report seems to imply that officials of the diocese had the same knowledge in the 1950s to 1980s as officials had in the late 1990s and they just did not act on this knowledge as they should until the late 1990s, when they were forced to do so.

Surely this is not possible. The whole country was on a learning curve during those years. Social workers told the commission that awareness and knowledge of child sexual abuse did not emerge in Ireland until about the early 1980s. The HSE told the commission that:

> In the mid 1970s there was no public, professional or government perception either in Ireland or internationally that child sexual abuse constituted a societal problem or was a major risk to children. (6.53)

Bishops, despite their position and inside knowledge of events in a diocese, are not gifted with knowledge and insights that are not available in society in general. Certainly, diocesan officials knew that there were cases of sexual abuse of children, as undoubtedly did the Gardaí and others. There are, however, other dimensions to the learning curve, none of which is simple:

1. Learning the extent of the abuse.
2. Learning to understand the gravity of the effects of child sexual abuse on the child. Few if any people knew then the depth and persistence of the damage done to a child by sexual abuse.
3. Learning to understand the mentality and modes of operation of any person who sexually abuses a child and his or her motivation and deviousness in the process.
4. Learning to devise the best way of assessing offenders, understanding the likelihood or not of the person re-offending whether with or without treatment and devising and implementing the best methods of treatment and the most effective ways of monitoring the offender afterwards.
5. The process of development of law and of getting a variety of agencies to communicate and work effectively together on the matter.

The report states:

> The taking out of insurance was an act proving knowledge of child sexual abuse as a potential major cost to the archdiocese and is inconsistent with the view that Archdiocesan officials were still 'on a learning curve' at a much later date, or were lacking in an appreciation of the phenomenon of clerical child sex abuse. (1.21)

Chapter 9 of the report deals with the matter of insurance in regard to child sexual abuse by clergy in the diocese. The fact that the initial premium in 1987 was the derisory sum of £515 (9.6), even granted the change in money values, shows clearly an amazing lack of appreciation of the gravity of the matter by the diocesan authorities and, indeed, by the insurance company. The report abounds in evidence of the learning process: paragraphs 1.16, 1.86, 4.54, 6.53 and all of Chapter 7 about the *Framework*

Document. Bishops are not exempt from the learning process.

Do we judge people, in the matter of things done ten/twenty/ thirty years ago, for not having acted according to the knowledge we now have? This has a bearing on the question of whether some course of action or inaction is 'inexcusable'. People knew sexual abuse of children was wrong; but without the current level of understanding of the appalling consequences for the abused person and of how difficult it can be to get an abuser to change, the practice then of treating it as no more than a moral failure (although serious) by the abuser is perhaps easier to understand. Thankfully, we know better today.

Learning continues. We are clear nowadays on the wisdom and advisability of referring allegations to civil authorities; clear procedures have been established. This was not the case twenty or thirty years ago. Then there was much debate among social workers about mandatory reporting and whether such a provision would inhibit complainants from seeking support or redress if they knew the issue had to be reported to the Gardaí.

To say there was a learning curve is not a 'get-out' clause. It does not mean nothing wrong was done. It does mean that we must take this factor into account in assessing the real level of responsibility and culpability for what was done. From the 1960s -1980s, how much attention, if any, was given to child sexual abuse in training for law? In training for psychiatry? In social work? In education? Psychologist Tony Bates writes[*] that in the 1979 edition psychology textbook he used, there was no mention of child sexual abuse. How much or little did our journalists, newspapers and media, our professional news-finders, know? What records did officials in health or sport or secular education keep? Clerical child abuse is a small percentage of the total. What was the received wisdom then, if any, about management and treatment and rehabilitation? Were there mismanagement or

---

[*] *The Irish Times* 'Health Plus', 8 December 2009.

concealment in other spheres and professions? We must address all abuse throughout society.

One might claim, as one journalist did to me: 'The media has a case to answer for its inaction where all of this was concerned. But they too had been in thrall to the power of Church authorities, which isn't surprising as most reporters/editors in the past were also educated by the Church.' I wonder what other journalists would say about that. It implies that those involved in the media had some knowledge of what was happening but failed to challenge the prevailing culture, due to being 'in thrall to the power of Church authorities'.

Did Those in Authority in the Diocese Have Collective Responsibility?

The Church, in this diocese at least, has not been conspicuous for practising collective responsibility. In my forty-two years of service, it has been more conspicuous by its absence. There can be no real collective responsibility unless contrary opinions can be openly expressed and valued. This is an area in which we need renewal. There is also the question of collective responsibility, not just within the Church, but with state and other relevant bodies.

How the Irish media have handled this may be instructive. We have seen concerted and persistent pressure on bishops to resign, based at least in part on their alleged failure in collective responsibility. Whether this collective responsibility was a reality needs to be established. By contrast, in the preceding months there was clear failure of collective responsibility in financial controls on the part of government and the governing boards of banks. There were calls for resignations but not, I suggest, as concerted or persistent as with the bishops. No member of government has resigned. Some senior members of bank management have resigned; many remain. Perhaps some investigative journalist would undertake to establish why there seem to have been two different standards in operation.

How Does the Law of the State Stand in Comparison with Church Law?

The report deals with Canon Law in Chapter 4. It gives no account of current civil law in this matter, except in relation to 'misprision of felony' (deliberate concealment of knowledge of a felony) in 5.35-5.39. The report states in 5.38-39: 'Relatively few of the complaints related to criminal charges that were classified as felonies at the time of the alleged commission of the offence.' Furthermore, the distinction between felonies and misdemeanours had been abolished by section 3 of the Criminal Law Act 1997. In the event, no file was sent to the DPP recommending prosecution for this offence.

Unless there are other provisions of civil law under which the abuse falls, it seems clear that the diocesan authorities did not put themselves above civil law in not reporting the cases to the Gardaí. The report states: 'There is no legal requirement for such reporting.' (1.16)

If few of the complaints were classified as felonies, it seems that civil law views child sexual abuse less seriously than Church law, as is evident from 1.2: Canon law and the procedures set out by the Roman Catholic Church for dealing with complaints of what Church law describes as the 'worst crime', that is, sexual interference with a minor. (This is corrected in 4.25, which makes it clear that the 'worst crime' covers a range of offences, including child sexual abuse.)

Any Other Reservations?

I have a question about the statement in 1.41 that Kevin McNamara was seriously ill when he was appointed archbishop in 1984. If this were the case, it would show a serious lack of pastoral care both for Kevin McNamara himself and for the diocese he was to serve. The good judgement of the Church is in question here. My information, which would need to be checked, is that he had had cancer before his appointment but that he had a medical check-up before he accepted. This gave him the assurance that, if the cancer did not recur within five years, there was no reason why he should not live a normal life-span. As we know, sadly, the cancer did recur.

Paragraph 1.96 reads:

> The Church did not start to report complaints of child sexual abuse to the Gardaí until late 1995. The commission notes that the Gardaí were happy with the co-operation they received from Archbishop Connell in 2002. For many complainants it was a gesture that came too late.

The closing sentence is disquieting. Certainly, it would have been better to take this step earlier; but to belittle it by calling it a 'gesture', as if it had little or no substance, is unworthy of this report which is so meticulous in other ways.

Where Can We Go from Here?

As Archbishop Diarmuid Martin has said repeatedly, Dublin diocese is in need of deep renewal. There are many possible ways to go about this. Some of the elements I would identify are as follows:

1. We must accept that the renewal will take time. Many people have felt anger at what the report reveals. We can use the information in the report, assess the conclusions of the commission in the light of remarks like those above and harness the anger into a positive force for renewal, rather than a destructive force.
2. The renewal will be personal, spiritual and theological, as well

as in the diocese as a community. Structural change alone is not renewal. Renewal will draw on the resources of the lay people and priests of the diocese. It cannot be a closed shop.

3.   It will develop ways in which challenge to prevailing culture is not just allowed but encouraged as an essential way of drawing on the resources of all members of the diocese. This cannot exclude challenging church authorities in the Vatican to greater faithfulness and effective pastoral care. This is a duty we owe in love. There must be love in facing the truth: *caritas in veritate*.

4.   It will involve a growing awareness of our woundedness. The power to grow in wisdom and grace must integrate what we celebrate at Christmas. Jesus changes our world and our hearts not with seven legions of angels but in the way the very weakness of a child can draw extraordinary love and compassion from the hearts of those around.

5.   It will, where possible, be done in close cooperation with other Christian churches. The sins we have witnessed in our diocese affect not just the abused and the perpetrators, nor indeed just the members of the Catholic church in our diocese. They wound all members of the Body of Christ, including those with whom we are not in full communion. They have been remarkable in their forbearance in not taking advantage of our failings but have been in their own way, a silent support. For this, I say 'Thank You'.

6.   This renewal will draw on the resources of those who have been most hurt by the abuses. Those who battled against such odds in bringing the truth to light when there were so many obstacles put in their way have made such renewal possible. Some may understandably have been so hurt that they will have nothing more to do with our diocese or church.

7.   Perhaps equally difficult will be to find how we can learn from those who were not themselves abused but who, in

the media and in other ways, have been forthright in their criticisms of the diocese and the Church. I have no doubt that we can discern the voice of the spirit in their words and actions also.

Conclusion

Diarmuid Martin, the Archbishop of Dublin, was under great pressure in the days and weeks after the publication of the report. What was (and still is) missing is a considered diocesan response. This is surprising, in view of the fact that we knew for some years that the report was coming.

I have attempted an objective review of the report, stating clearly what I find valuable and where I have reservations. Some of my reflections may bring a strong reaction. I have no mandate to speak for any other person. I hold no brief to defend the diocese, nor ways of exercising authority in the diocese or Church of which I have been critical for many years and which are an impediment to the mission of Jesus Christ I do not want to repair the damage done to the Church by the matters dealt with by *The Murphy Report*; rather, I want a renewed and rebuilt church, more faithful to its mission. As Kevin Kelly reminded us (*The Furrow*, December 2009): 'Vatican II remains an event in the future waiting to happen.' That mission may be summarised by what Luke (4:18)tells us of Jesus at the start of his mission, in the synagogue at Nazareth: 'The spirit of the Lord has been given to me…He has sent me to bring the good news to the poor…to set the downtrodden free…' By a divine paradox, in the matters which *The Murphy Report* covers, the downtrodden – those abused as children – have been the ones to set our diocese on the path to freedom. The last shall be first. We now need the wisdom and courage to set out on that path. We could make use of this year of Luke in the *Sunday Lectionary* to lay the foundations.

I have no monopoly of wisdom. Others may arrive at quite

a different assessment of the report. This I welcome. This is the debate we should be having, if we are to arrive at truth and reconciliation, at repentance and healing and forgiveness.

In a word, Resurrection. But first, the Cross.

Appendix V: Unintended Consequences*

People in positions of responsibility in business and banking and construction and politics, whose decisions and actions contributed directly to the current economic difficulties in Ireland and elsewhere, had no intention of bringing about those difficulties, or of destroying their own businesses. They were carrying out their work and making money. Some may have had misgivings at times, or even moral qualms, but they went ahead; now we have the consequences. Unintended consequences may result from someone driving home following several alcoholic drinks. And from bishops and others who were concerned for the reputation of the Church and of their priests. And from investigative journalists who go for a good story. All can be blinded by too narrow a focus on their own speciality and in the process may wreak havoc. If we fail to consider the consequences of our actions, we are on dangerous ground.

I am seriously concerned at what may be unintended damaging consequences of the ways media have reported on child sexual abuse in Ireland. Those same media have been remarkably effective in bringing to light terrible violations of vulnerable people, both in the abuse and in the way those in authority failed when confronted with that abuse. Without taking from that, we need to examine other consequences. RTÉ, the national public service broadcaster, is currently undergoing investigation in relation to *Prime Time Investigates* and *Frontline* programmes.

I intend to focus on print media, *The Irish Times*. This is not to suggest that this newspaper is particularly wayward. The exercise

---

* Published in *The Furrow*, May 2012

could be repeated with other parts of the public media. It is the newspaper with which I am most familiar (and for which I pay daily). I have two reasons for doing so. Firstly: In July 2003, the then editor, Geraldine Kennedy wrote on their website: 'We have moved in recent years from being the newspaper of record to the newspaper of reference...Our readers want access to the raw facts themselves and then they like to accept, or reject, our analysis of what they mean...When we get it wrong, we say so.' I suspect the current editor would share those aspirations. Since the newspaper aspires to be the 'newspaper of reference', to which historians in coming years may refer for reliable accounts, it is good to examine how this stands up.

Secondly: *The Irish Times* has an online archive search facility (on subscription), which facilitates this kind of study. The online search facility is helpful, although it cannot provide full results on its own. Other media may have similar facilities but I could not undertake a fully comprehensive survey. I hope others may be encouraged to do so.

On the subject of child sexual abuse, we have had in Ireland *The Ferns Report* (October 2005), *The Ryan Report* on abuse of children in institutions (May 2009), *The Murphy Report* on Dublin Diocese (November 2009) and *The Murphy Report* on Cloyne Diocese (July 2011). These reported shocking abuse and received wall-to-wall coverage in print and broadcast media. Remember the successive waves of outrage as these reports were published. Could anything be worse?

But imagine the outrage at an institution where 42 per cent of the female residents reported some form of sexual abuse (contact and non-contact) in their lifetime and where 28 per cent of the male residents made a similar report. This is not imagination. This is the situation in the institution we know as this state, the Republic of Ireland, as described on p. xxxiii of the *SAVI* (*Sexual Abuse and Violence in Ireland*) report of

April 2002 (executive summary). This report was carried out on behalf of Dublin Rape Crisis Centre by the Health Services Research Centre, Department of Psychology, Royal College of Surgeons in Ireland, and is available online. The Church reports are important; the findings of the comprehensive *SAVI* report provide the indispensable context. But do you remember any outrage in April 2002 when this report became public? Among your friends who know of Ferns, Ryan, Murphy and Cloyne, how many are in any way familiar with *SAVI*? A contributory reason for the absence of outrage after *SAVI* must be the level of reporting in the media. In March 2012, I checked the archive of *The Irish Times* for '*SAVI* report'. There was a news item (on the website) on 19 April 2002 but it does not mention the name of the report. The following day, a 608-word item tells of a conference in Dublin to launch the report but again does not mention the name of the report. The first reference to *SAVI* by name which appears in a search for '*SAVI* report' is on 24 June, under the heading 'Drink is the real rape problem'. The report is now ten years old. The search for '*SAVI* report' on *The Irish Times* archive shows forty-one items referring to it in those ten years. Ten of those articles were by columnist Vincent Browne; five were letters to the editor.

SAVI has been totally eclipsed by Ferns, Ryan, Murphy and Cloyne. *The Murphy Report* into the handling of abuse cases in the diocese of Dublin was published on 26 November 2009. On the following day there were thirty-five items dealing with the report (*Ferns*, 2005, had thirty-two). Where *SAVI* had forty-one articles in ten years, *The Murphy Report* had one hundred and seven in the first week. To make quite sure, I paged through the issues for each day online to spot the items, because many of the articles dealing with the report did not surface in the search results, probably because they did not contain the words *Murphy Report*. Comparison by word-count would be better but is beyond my capacity.

Why this extraordinary difference in reporting? Clearly a newspaper wants to publish stories which interest readers; but it is vital that the most important stories come to attention. Perhaps there is a perception that the *SAVI* Report, a survey dealing with the overall facts of abuse in Ireland, lacks punch and a clear target. In the report on 20 April 2002, there is one photograph of Dr Gill Mezey of London. On the other hand, *The Murphy Report* and the other church-related reports have a very clear target, a prominent institution which kept records. There were names and photographs aplenty to put with it. These are some of the dynamics of newspaper publishing and there may be other factors of which I am unaware. Michael Breen[*] quotes R.E. Cheit (2003): '...the cases (of child sexual abuse) that receive significant coverage are likely to follow a common pattern in crime reporting; one that exalts the unusual...These stories tended to involve 'the bizarre and the unusual', the dramatic and/or the famous'. Perhaps something here explains the extraordinary imbalance in reportage of clerical abuse.

Search results on the other reports to date show similar levels. I have not weeded out items which do not in fact refer to those reports but the number of results in a search from the report dates until the present give some indication: Ferns 216 results; Ryan 546, Dublin 488 and Cloyne 209. Repeat searches sometimes show slightly different results. With Ryan and Dublin, there is probably a larger proportion of spurious results due to the names Murphy and Ryan. Nonetheless, in this tsunami, *SAVI*'s forty-one are wiped out.

Michael Breen (p. 6) quotes B.C. Cohen (1963): '[The press] may not be successful much of the time in telling people what to think but it is stunningly successful in telling its readers what to think about.' Breen quotes M. McCombs and D. Shaw (1993):

---

[*] See note at the end of this article.

'Agenda setting is considerably more than the classical assertion that the news tells us what to think about. The news also tells us how to think about it.'

Finally: what kinds of words and labels are used and how do they reflect reality? According to an archive search from 1859, the first time the word 'paedophile' is used in *The Irish Times* is in an article by Maeve Binchy on 12 August 1975. Then follows the deluge: 1975 to 1995 – 477 hits; 1996 to 29 March 2012 – 2030 hits. The earliest reference I can find to sexual abuse of children is on 25 February 1971. The website archive search function may not be fully effective.

See what *SAVI* (p. xxxv) tells: 24 per cent of abusers of girls were family members; 14 per cent of abusers of boys were family members. (The 2010 Report of the Rape Crisis Network of Ireland says that of those who were subjected to a single incident of child sexual violence, 49 per cent were by a family member.) In one out of every four cases the perpetrator was another child or adolescent (seventeen or younger). Page 88 has a table showing the profile of abusers identified as being authority figures for those reporting child sexual abuse. As a proportion of all abusers, just 1.9 per cent of abusers of boys are described as 'religious minister' and 3.9 per cent as 'teacher (religious)'. Abusers of girls are 1.4 per cent 'religious minister' and 0 per cent 'teacher (religious)'. No denomination is specified.

Now compare those percentages with these search results of occurrences on *The Irish Times* archive, 1996–2012, first taking a general term and then adding 'priest' or 'clerical':

The term 'paedophile' occurs 2,030 times.

Of these:

416 (20.49%) have 'paedophile priest'; 4 (0.2%) have 'paedophile teacher'; 1 (0.05%) have 'paedophile doctor'.

The terms 'paedophile lawyer' and 'paedophile journalist' do not occur.

The term 'sex abuse' occurs 3114 times.

Of these, 554 (17.79%) have 'clerical sex abuse.'

'Child sex abuse' occurs 1570 times.

Of these, 657 (41.85%) have 'clerical child sex abuse.'

Without actually stating it, the use of language in this manner could convey the idea that clerics/priests are responsible for anything from 17-41 per cent of child sexual abuse. Neglect of *SAVI* information, disproportionate reporting of church reports and implicit demonising of Catholic clerics combine to produce unintended consequences. If this pattern is repeated across other print and electronic media, it may explain the results of the Iona Institute poll in November 2011, that a clear majority of the public overestimate the number of Catholic clergy who are guilty of child abuse.

On 6 November 2002, Helen Goode, one of the team who assisted with the *SAVI* report, asked in *The Irish Times*: 'How will society more generally address the 97 per cent of child sexual abuse, still largely hidden and not perpetrated by clergy?' Failure to address this is clearly the most damaging consequence of the *SAVI* report not receiving the attention it warrants.

One would hope that people versed in law are sufficiently expert not to be influenced by unbalanced media presentation. It could, however, be a contributory factor in some unbalanced statements in *The Murphy Report*, about which I wrote in *The Furrow*, February 2010. It could have affected the Minister for Justice, Alan Shatter, a solicitor, in his statement the day after the RTÉ *Prime Time Investigates* programme *Mission to Prey* in May 2011, which included false allegations about Father Kevin Reynolds. In his statement (still on the website of the Department of Justice), the Minister unguardedly used the word 'revelations' instead of 'allegations'*.

---

* 'I share the widespread public concern and disgust at the revelations which the programme contained.' www.justice.ie.

Unbalanced media reporting may facilitate 'the bizarre and the unusual' (see Cheit quotation above): we have 'Dutch Catholic-run institutions castrated boys for homosexual feelings' as a heading in *The Irish Times* (21 March 2012). The 505-word report then softens to 'may have been castrated'. A disturbing story; but, in targeting 'Catholic', it ignores the context of a eugenic mindset in many countries at the time: about four hundred 'therapeutic castrations' in the Netherlands 1938-1968; predominantly non-Catholic Sweden and Finland rank high in sterilisations of those considered deviant or feeble-minded, as do California and North Carolina.

I write of 'unintended consequences': I attribute no ill-will to those working in the media. The 'big story' can carry us all along. Because I am a Catholic priest, some may say I'm protecting the Catholic Church. This is true and the best way to do this is to acknowledge honestly the abuses and injustices for which some Catholics, lay and ordained, are responsible and to work for justice for all, regardless of faith affiliation.

Much more could be said. I have no professional expertise in this kind of study. The numbers I give are indicative, not definitive. If anyone can correct or add to or debunk my method or results, I will be glad to hear; especially, perhaps, someone from *The Irish Times*! Meanwhile, *SAVI* belatedly needs to receive urgent attention and be acted upon. We now have the experience of child protection in Church to provide lessons. We cannot guarantee that no child will be abused but failure to address the 97 per cent is not an option.

Note

For this article I drew on work by Michael Breen (then of the Department of Media and Communication Studies, Mary Immaculate College, Limerick). His essay, 'Through the Looking Glass: How the Mass Media Represent, Reflect and Refract

Sexual Crime in Ireland,' examines *The Irish Times* in detail, and makes some comparisons with RTÉ.

I also drew on work by a blogger who uses the pseudonym 'The Thirsty Gargoyle'. Two blogs in particular attracted my attention: 'Ireland Through a Glass Darkly' (2 August 2011) and 'A Dangerously One-Eyed View' (26 November 2011. This commentator examines reporting in *The Irish Times*.

At the time of writing, I was unable to carry out an examination of the *Irish Independent* as I did of *The Irish Times* because that newspaper's online archive was not yet complete.

When this article was published in *The Furrow* in May 2012, I sent copies to various prominent journalists but I can find no comment on it, or reference to it, in print or broadcast media

Index